DOING TIME
IN THE
PULPIT

DOING *TIME* IN THE PULPIT

THE RELATIONSHIP BETWEEN NARRATIVE AND PREACHING

Eugene L. Lowry

Abingdon Press
Nashville

Doing Time in the Pulpit

Copyright © 1985 by Abingdon Press

All rights reserved.

Library of Congress Cataloging in Publication Data

LOWRY, EUGENE L.
  Doing time in the pulpit.
  Bibliography: p.
  Includes index.
  1. Preaching. 2. Time (Theology) I. Title.
    BV4221.L678   1985   251   84-24383

ISBN 0-687-11034-3

MANUFACTURED BY THE PARTHENON PRESS AT
NASHVILLE, TENNESSEE, UNITED STATES OF AMERICA

Contents

To
my parents
Myrtle & Lynn Lowry
for my life's time

INTRODUCTION

Doing time! The phrase is apt. When a judge pronounces sentence upon any person, the central issue of confinement—the loss of human freedom—is not *where* but *how long*. Not space, but time—for time is how life is lived.

The phrase "Doing TIME in the Pulpit" refers not to a jail sentence, although preachers may wonder from time to time! The phrase refers to the connection between time and the sermon. Even when unnamed, the category of time underlies the current homiletical interest in narrative, story, parable, and plot. Time was the primary mode of Jesus' preaching, just as the Kingdom he announced is an inbreaking of a promised time.

Yet, most of us have been taught to work with *space* in the pulpit rather than moving with *time*; that is, we have been trained to execute a space-construction rather than facilitate a time-formation. Hence our current interest in narrative or story will turn to passing fancy—even be relegated to the anecdotal—unless experienced as an outgrowth of the category of time. When we hear *in time*, issues such as narrative, plot, story, parable, creativity, performative language, or even kairos find new connections and come alive. And so will our preaching! But the journey will not be easy.

The grammar of our native tongue gives precedence to nouns and hence to objects in space rather than to verbs and movement in time. Even as we talk motion, durée will petrify into space. I reach for the help of metaphor and the sense of it crumbles in my hand. For example, shall I say that this book is about *time* and time's possible impact upon a sermon that is riding upon its galloping back? In such a metaphor the sermon is sitting still and only the implied horse is moving. We could use the image of a sermon being caught up in the tide of the gospel, but still the sermon is a *thing* being carried. Truth is, the sermon *is* the horse; it *is* the tide.

The sermon is not a thing at all; it is an ordered form of moving time. This is in fact my thesis:

> *A sermon is an ordered form of moving time.*

In the following pages we are going to consider time and time's impact upon our practice of preaching. We will explore narrative art theory—focusing particularly upon the parabolic preaching of Jesus. We will consider the potentially creative connection between preparation time and the preached sermon.

We begin by noticing the difference between preaching that *orders ideas* and preaching that *orders experience*.

DOING *TIME*
IN THE
PULPIT

Chapter One

SERMON TIME AS THE ORDERING OF EXPERIENCE

You sit down at your desk to begin your sermon preparation for next Sunday. In front of you—or soon to be—are scribbled notes on paper, a Bible open to the lectionary passages for next Sunday, a magazine article on a subject you think might be appropriate, perhaps a commentary, and chaos! Disconnection is everywhere. You are nervous with the recognition that something must congeal soon, for once again Sunday is coming. But at the moment nothing is happening except the passing of time. Or so it seems.

Underneath the surface of your consciousness much is happening, even while you think it not so. The fact is, you are making powerful decisions about Sunday's sermon—decisions made more potent by the fact that they are hidden. Everything you ever learned in preaching lab, and before that in speech class, is busy at work. There is a system that you have worked countless times before—or a system that has worked you—and it is functioning. As Michael Polanyi puts it, we "know more than we can tell." And that *more* is at work.

An informing image of the term *sermon* is exerting its sovereign sway; yet that sovereignty is defended by honest innocence. If ever that system were brought to the surface, if the image were placed on the table of consciousness, it could by examination be voted out of power *or* returned to power—or any number of options in between. (The likely reason sermon workshops, seminars, and lectures often effect so little change in our preaching is not that the content of those

11

experiences "sounds fine, but just doesn't work in practice," as much as the fact that the experience did not really touch the undercover convictions behind our sermonic preparation.)

What I hope to have happen at this moment is to begin a process of getting in touch with that *more* that we know and cannot tell, even to ourselves. To commence the process of image examination (a process that once started will likely never stop), I want to explore a set of polarities placed in as "pure" a form as possible, that is, stated as either/or but known really to be a continuum. And while I hope you will think cognitively on these things with focused energy and intentionality, more importantly I hope you will allow the stated polar extremes to "age" in your consciousness. After all, unaccustomed to the light of day, images do have their defenses up, and their powerful meaning is as much "felt" as known. It is also difficult to perceive these elusive images through the several necessary angles of view (provided in sequence) when the first glance needs the fourth or fifth glance really to be clear. Nonetheless we will attempt (perhaps little by little) to see "where we are coming from" by way of unconscious systems.

Most of us were trained to think space and not time, unconsciously of course, when we sit down to begin sermon preparation. The result is that without conscious consent we immediately set about to order ideas. The textbook many of us used in seminary preaching classes is *The Principles and Practice of Preaching*, by Ilion T. Jones. Some of you will recall that green volume that identifies one of the key purposes of preaching: "to translate the Gospel into modern thought/terms."[1] Note the key terms: *ideas* and *thought*. The moment the mind engages this way we are placed in the world of space.

Although ideas are not corporeal like houses, yet a remarkable connection is made by our grammar. Nouns, you recall from English class, refer to persons, places and things—the stuff of space; whereas verbs on the other hand refer to action, movement, duration—elements of time. As it turns out grammatically, ideas have much more in common with things than with motion, and the primary choices are few. Ideas, if actual, are *there*—invisible things, if you please. Says philosopher Henri Bergson: "Language requires us to establish between our ideas the same sharp and precise distinctions, the same discontinuity, as between material objects." So W. E. Sangster's classic work is entitled *The Craft of Sermon Construction,* and the link with space becomes well defined indeed. Just recently I received a copy of a new book on preaching entitled *Building the Word.* The author, J. Randall Nichols, reflects on the title: "Where the image came from is a mystery." A few lines later he explains that in fact "people use these things we build to live in or work in or get well in."[2] Construction. Build. Live in. The image is strong, and it is spatial. Is it not true that when we juggle those notes we have on paper, we are doing something akin to architectual work—attempting to determine *where* the ideas *fit*? For our task is to have them properly *in place.*

Suppose instead, that rather than order ideas—spacing them, as it were—we imaged a sermon as *ordering experience.* Our attention immediately is drawn away from those ideas represented on paper and toward the congregation who will be listening next Sunday. Knowing their existence in time (actually several times), we now perceive our work as doing something with their twenty minutes of listening time. Sunday we will need to arrest their times and supplant them with another time—the sermon's.

Ideas seldom have the power to supplant time; a story seldom fails. Perhaps this is why we were admonished to begin a sermon with an illustration. But alas it was too often temporary (sometimes inconsequential) and soon we were back turning out ideas with our space machine. This is not to suggest that experience has no ideational content nor vice versa. It is to pinpoint our primary attention. A moving sermon is more like a trip that takes us from here to there through the medium of time—from now to then. Is it any wonder that Jesus "did not speak to them without a parable"

(Mark 4:34). So the "righteous" man asked: "And who is my neighbor?" (Luke 10:29). That is, Who has a claim upon my time and energy?—a philosophical, ideational question if ever there was one. Jesus could have said: "There are several important ideas regarding 'neighbor' that ought to be discussed. First . . ." In which case the man whose defenses were up would have listened—just long enough to start framing his next query. Instead, Jesus replies: "A man was going down from Jerusalem," (Luke 10:30), and the man doesn't know what to defend against. His time is being supplanted. He is jerked from propositional question to storytime, and before he knows what to do he is halfway down the road to Jericho. Certainly the ideas are there—couched in the story—and he is left to ponder. But sometimes the biblical redactors were concerned lest we miss the moral, so they explained it (and often ruined it). Almost never are following explanatory passages the genuine words of Jesus. The parables are one form of ordering experience in time, instead of ordering ideas in space. (I will suggest others in the chapter on narrative time.)

The Task: To Organize or to Shape

Moreover, the preparation *task* of ordering ideas is altogether different from that of ordering experience. It is the difference between *organizing* and *shaping*.

Ilion T. Jones was an organizer (and by reputation, a very good one). His first rule: "To attain unity each point should be a subthesis of the main thesis."[3] His test to see if the unity has been accomplished consists of writing "the theme of the sermon as a complete sentence, a fully stated proposition. Then . . . write out each point on a separate line. . . . Does each point constitute a distinct phase of the thesis? Is each point subordinate to the main thesis?"

Behind this advice (which is quite sound if one wants to order ideas) is an assumption, perhaps even an admission. One speaks of *attaining unity* only when one assumes it is not already there. There is something independent about the parts of the sermon, and these parts need to be glued together. And of course ideas fit just such a picture. If one has several ideas, each of which can be stated in a complete sentence, then a means of bridging the independent parts is required. Fred Craddock speaks of the typical result—that "some sermons were three sermonettes barely glued together."[4] But another result ensues that most of us have experienced with some discomfort. Various pieces standing alone make movement very difficult. There is nothing that can close down attention more easily than a complete thought. Once a proposition is stated, it is done; closure has occurred, and only with great difficulty can one get things moving again. Often the sermon *looks* good in the study but *sounds* as if it was contrived piece by piece in the pulpit. We juggle and fumble for a way to go on. But there is a larger problem yet.

It is the problem of control. The image of ordering ideas assumes a resultant mastery. One gets the truth in place, declares it, puts it into a proposition. Putty in one's hands. The matter is closed—even if the preacher does not intend such a result. The issue is parallel to the one addressed by James M. Robinson and others of the new hermeneutic school of thought. They are rightly concerned that we as workers with Scripture seem by definition to call the shots. We think we are in control of explaining, apprising, and defining. Is it not the other way around, they ask? The Scripture addresses us—explaining, apprising, and defining. It is we who need figuring out, not the Bible. The same problem confronts us when we deal with any kind of ideas. And one wonders, is there a way to approach our task that is less influenced by our urge to control?

It is to see our task as *shaping* rather than *organizing* sermons. H. Grady Davis identifies the important difference when he notes that a sermon is "like a tree," which is a "living organism."[5] When *task* is imaged as *pruning* rather than *building*, we are placed in the role of servant.

I have been impressed with the constant witness of writers

15

either whom I have met personally or whose reflection on their own art I have read. Inevitably they report how little they knew about a story's conclusion when they began writing. Madeleine L'Engle knew that Meg and Charles would return safely, before they even left, in the Newberry Award science fiction novel *Wrinkle in Time*, but she didn't know *how* it could happen. In the process of writing, "you just have to listen to the story," she told me. Frederick Buechner reported that, in *Lion Country*, when he had Antonio set out for Florida, he (Buechner) did not know Antonio would fall in love. "I try to stay in the company of the character," said he. In *Walking on Water*, L'Engle explains: "When the work takes over, then the artist is enabled to get out of the way, not to interfere. When the work takes over, then the artist listens." But, how? How does one listen and *shape* rather than control and *organize*?

First, one attends to *movement* rather than *thought*. If early in our preparation we concentrate on the congregation's future experience of the sermon, typically we will have a beginning or an ending—not the whole sermon form at that point. Moving either forward or backward we begin the experiential journey. Some would advise organizing the whole first, then filling it in, but *shaping* a sermon suggests the reverse. Craddock advises working inductively rather than deductively. One helpful way is to ask small, concrete questions, rather than large ones, early in preparation. Concern yourself with eggs first, then baskets—not the other way around.

For example, in working on a parable I violate what I was taught, namely to first figure out the central meaning of the story. If I do that first, creativity will shut down and I have little opportunity to listen. Rather, I will walk through a portion of the story, placing myself in the shoes of the several different characters. I even role-play the scene out loud. It is almost free association. Ideas that I would never have considered while standing outside the story begin to happen to me while inside. Only after these experiences am I ready to shape the whole. Perhaps you recall the time you intended to use an illustration to concretize your main point—but after telling yourself the illustration, you discovered that it really told a more important point than you had in mind for it. And your sermon had to be altered to accommodate it.

The point is, such work with the specific ingredients of experience allows a more open-ended process of preparation. The larger issue of shaping has to do with plot (which we will address shortly). If our task, then, is either to organize or to shape, what is the *form* that ensues?

The Form: A Structure or a Process

Those who *order ideas* and whose task therefore is to *organize* will find their sermon form to be a *structure*. Those who *order experience* and whose task therefore is to *shape* will find their sermon form to be a *process*.

The difference is grasped easily if one imagines a complete set of sermon notes. Do they look like an office building or a map? Do they appear to move vertically or horizontally? When the notes are read, do they have the feel of referring to *this* and *this* and *this*, or to *then* and *then* and *then*? The former case reflects a sermon structure. Of course it would look like an office building because in fact construction or building is the central image behind it. On the other hand, a sermon process moves in a more linear fashion because life is experienced in time.

Another key difference is the grammar of central points— either top to bottom or on the way. In the sermon *structure* the central points tend to have the finality of propositional statement. In a sermon *process* the important "points" have the feel of transition, like necessary road markers that must be heeded if one is going to arrive at the proper destination. In fact a sermon structure will be marked by a declarative statement; a sermon process often will be marked by a question. Again, structure often uses interchangeable points, whereas process road markers are by necessity in series. "Chicago, 120 miles," then "Chicago, 180 miles" would mean real trouble for the traveler.

James S. Stewart was a master at sermon structure, and his sermon "The Gospel of the Ascension" is a good example of his work. His points are as follows:

1. It [Christ's ascension] was expedient for the spiritualizing of religion.
2. It was expedient for the universalizing of the gospel.
3. It was expedient for the energizing of evangelism.
4. It was expedient for the fortifying of faith.[6]

Note that point number two could just as easily have been number three. The grammar has the finality of propositional statement. It has the feel of *this* and *this* and *this*. One has to import a reason for the points being in the chosen order: the ones which come to mind are (1) for purpose of climax, (2) in order of importance, (3) chronologically, or (4) from general to close-at-hand. In whatever case, the rationale for the chosen order is imported from outside the sermon itself.

After a dramatic shift of sermon style, Edmund A. Steimle became a master of sermon process. Although it is difficult to "outline" his Christmas Eve sermon, "The Eye of the Storm,"[7] I shall try to provide the chief road markers:

1. Hurricane Hazel's destruction at mid-point—the eye of the storm.

2. The first Christmas Eve too—between Old Testament flood and Crucifixion.

3. Tonight—Christmas Eve, between violence in Northern Ireland and the precarious future.

4. Tonight we celebrate the calm and rejoice. "All is calm, all is bright."

None of these points could be interchanged. The story of Hurricane Hazel is absolutely necessary for his re-imaging of the first Christmas Eve, which in turn redefines the present moment and its call to rejoice. It is not structure, but process; it is more indicative than imperative.

The Focus: Theme or Events

So therefore, the preacher who orders ideas into a structural form will *focus on a theme*, while the preacher who orders experience into a process form will *focus on events*. The first kind of sermon work will look for a unifying ideational thread. For Stewart that thread was the term "expedient." In other words the Ascension makes sense, its importance being seen in the way it prompts such consequences as universalizing the gospel, fortifying faith, and so forth. Steimle's sermon focused on events that taken serially (horizontally/historically) alter one's grasp of the present. Hurricane Hazel provides the image for the biblical flashback to the birth of Christ—now seen afresh, which in turn names the meaning of this Christmas Eve. The great power of Steimle's sermon is identified by Giles Gunn's description of the effect of language upon experience: "Life suddenly releases some of its unspent force, and conventional expectations and interpretations are toppled by the flood of new insight and illumination."[8]

In conversation with Frederick Buechner in the spring of 1981, this difference between focusing on theme and focusing on event was summarized powerfully when he said:

> I think many people who know I am a minister writing a novel assume that I start out with some specifically Christian theme or message which I then dream up a story to illustrate with characters and dialogue to help. That's not the case at all. Insofar as there is such a theme it emerges through the events that take place and the interaction of the characters.[9]

The Principle: Substance or Resolution

Throughout the process of sermon preparation we not only are busy with the work itself, we keep a portion of our consciousness free to assess how we're doing. There are key moments when we literally stop our preparation time to judge our progress, to see if it is happening the way we want. But even in between we keep a kind of automatic eye out for indication of false moves, unproductive detours. Although we never may have consciously formulated them as such, we are utilizing norms for judgment, tests that result in red and green lights for our work. So that when our preparation is interrupted by another's question, "How are you doing on the sermon?" we know immediately how to answer. Our monitoring system is alert, and we feel it in our bones. But what are the norms? On what basis do we know how we are doing?

Under the surface of consciousness there is a principle at work that judges our efforts. If we have been taught by precept and experience to order ideas, most likely that principle is *substance*. Are we getting *it* said? Is a sufficient amount of properly organized content going to be relayed from pulpit to pew on Sunday? Or as Andrew Blackwood would ask it: "Does every part of it reveal what it should reveal?"[10]

On the other hand if you are busy ordering experience, the underlying principle is not substance but *resolution*. If the sermon is intended to intersect listeners' time and you are shaping a process of events, the question is finally: are you going to get through to the destination of resolution? Because of the nature of narrative the question one likely might ask, however, is not as easy as it seems. One might think that the question of how one is doing could easily be answered on the basis of whether with each step of the process the sermon seems to be closer to the destination. But narrative trips are different from car trips in that often resolution increasingly becomes more remote and difficult, *apparently*, until by some strange shift or move the resolution happens with utter surprise (we are after all dealing with time-based issues and their resolution rather than geographic trips). The prodigal, for example, was "closer" to home while living it up in the city than later when he wound up in the pig pen. But only through the further distancing between father and son could the return trip happen with power. We will examine this peculiar aspect of narrative process more in the next several chapters. At this point what is crucial is to sense the difference between the test by means of the principle of *substance* and the test by means of the principle of *resolution*. Also we will note a critical problem that emerges when substance is the underlying principle.

"What a preacher believes about the mode of divine revelation determines the mode of his preaching,"[11] said Canon Browne. He explained further: "Those who hold that divine revelation is given in propositional form will regard preaching as the statement of doctrine in a series of propositions expressed in definable terms." Of course those who don't, won't. Except Browne observes with keen perception that there are many of us who would not want to define revelation as propositional truth who yet preach as though we did. Hence "the form of their sermons denies implicitly what they state explicitly about the mode of revelation."

Now this is most peculiar. How can we account for such contradiction? Would we be so hypocritical in our ministry as this suggests? No, I think not. Browne has just presented us with a remarkably clear picture of the power of our homiletical image. It matters not that at the conscious theological level we affirm revelation in other than or beyond propositional terms. If we have internalized an image of preaching as the ordering of ideas and dutifully focused on our theme until its structure is properly organized, then we arrive at the pulpit with the Word propositionalized. Nor does it mean that professorial chairs in preaching are occupied only by those who insist on the literal inspiration of the Scriptures. It means that homiletical theory has drawn heavily upon the principles of rhetoric and unwittingly borrowed a principle that is not altogether suitable for our task. After all, "rhetoric is concerned with the ordering of ideas" (John E. Jordan in *Using Rhetoric*). Which presumes of course that the ideas in fact can be so ordered. But is the activity of God, God's time as

21

it breaks into ours, so neatly definable? If Dan Otto Via is right that the Bible "is to a large extent non-propositional,"[12] and if Robert Roth is correct that "truth is greater than the word of language,"[13] then imaging our work as ordering ideas and then testing them by the principle of substance not only falls short of our homiletical goal, but may in fact misdirect our efforts. The great preacher John Henry Jowett believed in ordering ideas and certainly wanted to test them on the basis of substance. In fact he thought every sermon should be reducible to a one-sentence summary:

> "I have a conviction that no sermon is ready for preaching, nor ready for writing out, until we can express its theme in a short, pregnant sentence as clear as crystal. . . . This is surely one of the most vital and essential factors in the making of a sermon."[14]

Browne, on the other hand wants to order experience, even likens the sermon to poetry, and objects to such reducible summaries:

> But is the meaning of a poem or sermon capable of being put in one single sentence? To what one unambiguous sentence could a Christmas sermon be reduced . . . If all that a sermon or a poem said could be put in one sentence, would there be any point in making sermons or poems?[15]

The Product: An Outline or a Plot

Our sermon preparation finally results in something taken into the pulpit (either on paper or at least in the head) depending on the conscious and subconscious convictions with which we work. If the preacher is ordering ideas, the resultant structural form likely will be an *outline*. If the preacher is ordering experience the resultant process form is a *plot*.

The venerable outline of a sermon is easily identifiable for us all. We are so familiar with it that little needs to be said, except to observe that it is utterly true to the informing image of preaching it represents. It is the epitome of organization, of structure, of substance. We are so accustomed to working with it that even when we are ordering experience we tend to press the outline into service—or rather, we try to force the process into outline form. Occasionally a keen ear can detect the struggle going on between meat and bones; sometimes we feel the guilt of failure, thinking we have good material but somehow it will not get into Roman-numeraled place. Rather than failure, the issue may be a mismatch of content and form. Perhaps our informing image does not, should not, result in an outline. Craddock describes the reverse result—when we have our complete set of outline notes in hand, arrive at the middle of the sermon presentation, know something is not working, and depart from the notes. "Some have even felt guilty about the departure," he notes, but the mismatch of content and form requires something to give.

Because most of us have been influenced by the tradition of rhetoric rather than the tradition of narrative composition, the notion of *plot* as sketched on paper may seem unfamiliar and difficult. Actually its use—if not its definition—is really simpler than an outline.

Aristotle says a plot is a "structure of events." Edwin Muir, in *The Structure of the Novel*, explains that "the term plot . . . designates . . . the chain of events in a story and the principle which knits it together."[16] Elizabeth Dipple expands the definition, indicating that the concept of plot goes "beyond scene or incident and accounts . . . for the movement of mind or soul."[17]

At this point the key issue is to note that a plot deals with some kind of *sequential ordering*, and typically includes an opening conflict, escalation or complication, a watershed experience (generally involving a reversal) and a denouement (that is, the working out of the resolution). In my earlier writing, *The Homiletical Plot*, I describe the five typical movements of a sermonic plot. But enough for now. We will explore *plot* in detail in chapter 4, "Narrative Time."

The Means: Logic and Clarity or Ambiguity and Suspense

Whether or not the outline that orders ideas "holds water" for us is determined by our judgment about the means: the logic and clarity of its component parts *and* their interrelationships. Sub-theses must be both subordinate to the main thesis and coordinate (or equal) with each other. I am using the term *logic* not in its technical sense but in the more general usage. I mean, does it make sense? Is it well reasoned, or does it feel contrived, superficial, or even illogical? What is clear, however, is that the means of logic and clarity have an ideational referent. We would be organizing ideas, after all. So the question of cognitive coherence is central. But the means of plot are ambiguity and suspense.

Says Wesley Kort in *Narrative Elements and Religious Meaning:* "An artist first is a responder to: situation, need, vacancy, chaos, enemy, evil," and the reader (or listener) "comes to the act with some lack, some deficiency.[18] Hence, the test of means is whether ambiguity based on discrepancy is maintained successfully until the preacher is ready to resolve matters with the gospel. Rather than cognitive coherence being central, the focus is on the question of correspondence—that is, does the ambiguity and/or suspense maintained by the preacher resonate as real as the listeners experience life? Can one identify with the characters and the action?

Now very quickly it can be perceived that often what is "good" for the outline is "bad" for the plot—and vice versa. For example, clarity of purpose in an outline is considered important and should be presented in some form in the introduction. But if it is ambiguity you are trying to maintain, you certainly would not want to let the cat out of the bag. Likewise, ambiguity is often taken for imprecision by followers of the outline method. What is appropriate is utterly dependent upon the informing image of one's work, whether ordering ideas or ordering experience.

The Goal: Understanding or Happening

Since preaching is so fundamental to ministry as we understand it (those who disagree are not likely to be reading this), surely we all ought to be able to provide a statement of the primary goal of preaching. Such an assignment in one sense would be quite easy. The title of James S. Stewart's classic volume, *Heralds of God*, might do quite nicely, or some statement about announcing what God has done through the Incarnation, or something about calling people to Christ—depending on our various theological persuasions. "Proclaiming the Word" might be a phrase broad enough to include us all—unless one is asked precisely what this means. The homiletical differences, theological disagreements and, if we were to admit it, inner uncertainties begin to take over with the result that venturing such statements would become a most perilous enterprise. Still, placed in the scope of broad, basic purpose, we all seem to be about the same task.

Strange then, that there seems to be an identifiable division among preachers regarding the primary goal of preaching—at least as it is discernible in practice. Stranger yet, the division does not follow the lines of theological camps or of homiletical traditions. It is the difference between those whose sermons appear to place highest priority on cognitive conceptualization and those whose sermons do not. I believe it an unconscious goal, based on the hidden image of the sermon. Those who order *ideas*, virtually disregarding their theological positions, will have *understanding* as the bottom line—whether the next step in the worship service is an altar call or the Eucharist, whether the content of the sermon is focused on spiritual growth or social action, and whether it is a biblical exposition or topical sermon without a text. Likewise, those who order *experience*—again whether of neo-orthodox, liberal, fundamentalist, or liberation persuasions—will move toward some kind of *happening*.

Steimle, Niedenthal, and Rice, in *Preaching the Story*, note that most of us operate from within one of four views of preaching.[19] It is interesting that all four views center on the goal of understanding. The first view focuses upon self-expression, and here Phillips Brooks' famous claim that "preaching is the communication of truth by man to men" is cited. Note the emphasis upon truth. The second view of preaching concentrates on the gathered community in which "effective communication" will "show how the resources of the Christian tradition set the needs and/or resolve the problem." The third view centers on institution and sees preaching as focused on persuasion, based in part on offering "the perspective life on God's terms." The fourth view states it head on: "The content or message of preaching."

But with all the differences of these four views, ideational content is yet central to them all, one way or another. But when the writers turn to their own view of the goal of preaching, the difference is startling: "Anyone who has experienced preaching, whether in pulpit or pew, knows that it is an event—a moment, a sudden seeing."

And so it is, when preaching is viewed as ordering experience. Says Buechner: "So if preachers . . . are to say anything that really matters . . . they must say it . . . to the part of us where dreams come from . . . , the inner part where thoughts mean less than images, elucidation less than evocation."[20]

Now that we have taken the time to concentrate on these two polar extremes which, if I am correct, rise from the power of our hidden image of the sermon, let us do the other task I suggested earlier: allow these extreme polarities to "age" in our consciousness. I am going to list below the key terms of our discussion, and ask you simply to look at them (left to right—top to bottom), feel the words, sense where it is that you resonate in practice and in hope.

SERMON TIME AS THE ORDERING OF EXPERIENCE

The Ordering
of

IDEAS   *EXPERIENCE*

The

IDEAS	The	EXPERIENCE
ORGANIZE	TASK	SHAPE
STRUCTURE	FORM	PROCESS
THEME	FOCUS	EVENTS
SUBSTANCE	PRINCIPLE	RESOLUTION
OUTLINE	PRODUCT	PLOT
LOGIC/CLARITY	MEANS	AMBIGUITY/SUSPENSE
UNDERSTANDING	GOAL	HAPPENING

As I indicated earlier, once the informing image—the unconscious system—is brought to consciousness, each of us can indeed choose to return it to power, throw it out of office, or choose some other option in between. It is obvious that I am not neutral in this matter, for I believe that the image of ordering ideas has had the lion's share of affirmation in recent homiletical history; I am convinced that many of us have intended to go about our task of ordering experience but have been prevented from doing so by the weight, shall we say, of preachers' "collective unconscious"; and I am persuaded that in spite of this "undercover influence" of ordering ideas, when we do well in the pulpit often it is when we lay aside our outlines of space and begin talking to our people in time.

In order to know how to move from ordering ideas to ordering experience, to shift from outlines of space to talking in time, we need help. Fortunately, help is available from those who have been ordering experience for a long, long time. Our colleagues the storytellers, the narrative artists—including Jesus—can become important models forus as we move from the *space* of rhetoric to the *time* of narrative art.

But first we must pause briefly to ask what appears to be a very simple question: *What is time?*

Chapter Two

THE TIMES OF OUR LIFE

I glance at my watch to check the time—and unconsciously live out Frederick Jameson's statement that time is "the way we live the world."[1] We are indeed temporal creatures; as Thomas Mann put it, time is "the medium of life."[2]

On the rare days when I mistakenly leave the house without my watch, I feel naked and lost. Because "there is no experience . . . which does not have a temporal index attached to it." I need my watch—to stay in touch.

If, as according to Meyerhoff, time is the "characteristic mode of our experience,"[3] then the sermon—if it is to be more than a report about life—must not simply talk *about* time, it must exist *within* it. That is why the issues of the previous chapter are so crucial to us as preachers. Ordering experience allows (or is it *requires*?) us to stay in touch with time, whereas ordering ideas tends to stop the clocks. If Ernst Cassirer is correct that "organic life exists only insofar as it evolves in time," then "timeless truths" also may turn out to be lifeless as well, and the sermon so framed will simply stand there in space while our listeners hear in time.

The deadening result is explained by David Buttrick, who noted the tendency of preachers to utilize what he called a "method of distillation."[4] He illustrated the problem by referring to the typical potential sermon one is likely to hear when the text is Luke 7:2-10—the story of the centurion's slave, whose master sees himself as unworthy but who knows authority when he sees it, and who implores Jesus to just "say the word." Buttrick proceeds with what we have come to expect:

> Usually, he [the preacher] approaches the passage as if it were objectively "there," a static construct from which he may get some*thing* to preach on. Either he will grab one of the verses—"Say the word," "I am not worthy," "he loves our nation, and he built us our synagogue"—treating the verse as a topic, or he will distill some general theme from the passage, for example, "the intercession of friends," "the compassion of Jesus," "an example of humility." Notice, in either case the preacher treats the passage as if it were a still-life picture in which some*thing* may be found, object-like to preach on. What has been ignored? The composition of the "picture," the narrative structure, the movement of the story, the whole question of what in fact the *passage* may want to preach. Above all, notice that the passage has been treated as a stopped, objective picture from which something may be taken out to preach on![5]

There is one word Buttrick did not use in his analysis, but it reverberates throughout his critique: *time*! It was time that was distilled *out* of the text.

My old-fashioned sweep-hand watch is very simplistic. Right now it says 2:37 but it doesn't know A.M. from P.M., or one day from the next. Mechanically speaking, any twelve-hour segment is the same as any other. My watch literally goes in circles—just like the time experienced by primitive societies. For them "the year is divided by the equinoxes and solstices which mark the sun's annual progress through the heavens and serve as indicators of seasonal variations."[6] Life was seen as circles of time within circles of time. The Greeks, too, thought in circles. So the player on the stage of life has a few days, and another player will have more of the same. Of course, if *chronos* is in fact chasing its tail (like my watch), history has little ultimate significance.

It appears, however, that the Hebrew-Christian tradition is largely responsible for declaring that my watch does not have the final word on time. Scholes and Kellogg explain that "the annual cycle of fertility ritual becomes, with the progressive concept of time which informs Jewish and Christian sacred myth, a linear spiral with a beginning and an end: the death-which-is-birth at the end of the spiral being the counterpart of the birth-which-is-death that begins it." Erich Frank, in *Philosophical Understanding and Religious Truth*, observes that "with Christianity . . . the Greek magic cycle of time has been broken! It is transformed into a straight line which leads into the future towards a definite goal."[7]

But my watch does not understand the tremendous implications of all this (to which we will need to return), it just moves along with regularity. Whether cyclical or linear, this is *chronos* time, "objective" enough that tonight's newspaper can tell us when to expect the "sun to rise" (an interesting way to put it, to be sure). But, then, Madeleine L'Engle, contemporary prize-winning writer of children's stories and lay theologian, asks: "How long is a toothache? How long is a wonderful time?" And we know that *chronos* is not all we mean when we talk about time.

Vividly I remember how long that last year was before I got my driver's license. I thought heaven and earth would pass away before my birthday rolled around. Time would hardly move at all. Now I can resonate with Frederick Buechner, who told me he had "crawled more than half way toward my death"—except that my crawl is picking up speed with every year. Immediately I know my watch is now utterly useless in considering this *inner time*.

Inner time, or *duration as subjective experience,* is ever at odds with the clock. The stall of experienced time at the occasion of unexpected loss or the sprint of ecstasy's day seems so utterly unique that we never fail to tell others about them—as if only we had ever "violated" time so remarkably.

Strangely, we often remember bad events as long and good events as short in duration, but this is not always the case. A good marriage is often reported as both an instant and forever—that is, an instant as time is moving so quickly, and forever in the sense of being unable to remember prior to the relationship. But the issue for us is not the long or the short of it.

The point is: within each of us there is an inner clock utterly unlike the watch on our wrists, and which mediates our experiences in the space-time world. It helps determine our capacity to process space-time experiences and in turn is shaped by them. Whenever a sermon happens—even if all watches were synchronized—the experience is shaped by the fact that there are as many inner clocks as there are listeners—all ticking at different speeds. Moreover, it is possible through the means of powerful narrative for these many inner clocks to begin to merge into synchronized harmony. Anyone who has ever filed out the exit door of a theater or a movie exclaiming how fast the time inside had gone knows that both chronological and inner times can be transcended and transformed by the power of narrative time. This goal is precisely the purpose of this writing. Later on we shall explore the power of metaphor, parable (as extended metaphor), and story in the remarkable reshaping of our time. For now, it is enough to note that *chronos* is not the only time. Inner time is another time. And then of course there is *kairos* time.

You are a resident of Kansas City, Missouri. It is July 17, 1981 (*chronos* time), and you are a little at odds with yourself and the world. It has been a long day (inner time). You decide to get away from life's troubles and attend the tea dance at the Hyatt Regency Hotel. You hear a crack like lightning and look up frozen in fright as concrete, steel, glass, and human bodies shower down in slow motion (actually the way many reported it). In an instant your life passes by in your mind until you feel the thrust of someone shoving you out of the way of instant death. But that someone was not so lucky. Life is transformed.

Kairos time—meaning literally "the *right time*." It is not so much a different *kind* of time as it is an *event* in time, which implodes two or three other kinds of time. Typically, kairos (1) involves an interaction among an exterior event, one's inner time, and chronological time; (2) includes the sense of duration being temporarily suspended (even unselfconsciousness about time's passing); and (3) results in some type of profound impact.

Or again, you go to see *Ordinary People*, thinking it will be a good escape from a harried day. Your inner time is taken over by the gripping plot, and the sense of *chronos* virtually disappears. While viewing this story of others' lives you begin to sense that on the screen *your* very own past is being relived, and you discover the *you* you never quite knew. It is a moment so profoundly sacred that in describing the experience to others you can only use the term *revelation*.

The liturgy of the church is intended to be and do precisely this. Liturgy is a reenactment of the story of salvation, and we are there. Even history so far past it is counted in centuries becomes *now*—the right time—kairos. Is it any wonder that when the youngest child of the Jewish family asks at the Seder ceremony: "Why is this night different from all other nights?" the answer is put in the historical present, not the simple past tense: "*We* were slaves . . . " H. Richard Niebuhr calls such a revelation the "Story of our Life." And to reenact it is to prompt kairos. Yet . . .

The term "*revelation*" and the illustration drawn from the Hyatt Regency tragedy raise a critical question here of the connection between kairos and the activity of God in human time. Is it to be presumed that *kairos* and *providence* are to be considered synonymous terms—or at least inextricably linked? Certainly the Hebrews viewed the Exodus as more than a happy coincidence. And the person saved from death by another's push at the Hyatt Regency is certainly likely to speak of that kairos event as God's doing (although the relatives of those who perished may well raise difficult questions!). And, what about the person who found the movie *Ordinary People* as a revelation?

This is not the place or time for attempted resolution of the questions of providence! Yet, we do need to be clear in sorting and defining the various forms of time, that the community of faith needs another category besides *kairos* for talking about God's advent in human history. Kairos as the *right time* may

33

indeed be utilized in describing a birthday party, and *flash of insight* may be a quite adequate way of speaking generally about revelation. In short, kairos may or may not include an assumption about God's activity. But when Niebuhr speaks of revelation, he does presume the activity of God (and we are free to argue the whens and wheres and hows, but not the *ifs*).

Obviously, we need another term to identify these events-in-time that the community of faith declares to be revelational and providential. How do we name that moment when *chronos* is turned to kairos by God? I am choosing the term *God's time*.

The truth is that *chronos* running nude through the ages is both too much and too little. It is too much in the sense of Patricia Tobin's objection to the oppressive company it keeps:

> It is no accident that the concept of linear time should be as intimate and peculiar an aspect of Western civilization as patriarchalism: the prestige of cause over effect, in historical time, is analogous to the prestige of the father over the son. Both initiate a time that may be imagined as an unidirectional and irreversible arrow, whose trajectory is determined by an original intention.[8]

It is too little in the sense of ultimate possible meaning. When one has all his or her eggs in *chronos'* basket, a relentless optimism or an unlimited pessimism often emerges. If you agree with Thomas Mann, that "time is related to—yes, identical with everything creative and active, every progress toward a higher goal," then your view of history is locked into an "onward and upward" expectation. On the other hand, Charles Baudelair, in *Les Fleurs Du Mal*, sees time conversely: "Time devours our lives, and the dark Enemy who knows us seems to fatten on our heart's blood and grow the more." Or again: "Time is a voracious gambler who wins at every throw," and "we are crushed every moment by the idea and sensation of time."

Pinning high hopes on *chronos* alone, whether it issues in wishful thinking or paralyzing despair, results in a dependency upon what Yeats called "the cracked tune that chronos sings." Although one can conceive of the moving of time toward some preordained fulfillment—good or bad or neither—chronos time in the Scripture is not just chronos. Says Norman Perrin: "In the Old Testament, time is punctiliar. . . . They thought in a linear manner only in the sense that they put together the sequence of events in which God had acted." Moreover, "With the coming of the prophets something new is added. . . . They claim that his hand is also *and equally* at work in the events of their own day." Finally, "They proclaim a future and even climactic salvation activity of God on behalf of his people."[9]

Apparently God will not leave chronos alone, and the Christian community continues to acknowledge the intrusion of God's time upon or within planet earth. Whether in the form of Dodd's realized eschatology, Bultmann's existential apocalypse, Crossan's advent of Being or even the Rapture folks' driverless car, they all hold this one conviction in common: *chronos* is not the last word.

Preaching, occurring as it does in *chronos*, announces God's time, which does not move in simple juxtaposition to *chronos* but indeed transforms it or names it, or announces it for what it is rather than what we thought it was. I believe L'Engle correct in saying that God's time "breaks through chronos with a shock of joy" but incorrect in saying that God's time "has nothing to do with chronological time." Again, surely Crossan is on target in noting that "one's authentic and primordial time does not come from the ticking of clocks and the wheeling of stars"; yet his additional statement that the advent of being "destroys one's planned projections"[10] may be misunderstood as a negation of chronological time. *Chronos* is, after all, a part of God's creation. To borrow Niebuhr's options relative to culture, it is not Christ *against* time, but Christ *transforming* time. The goal of every sermon is to effect that transformation—to prompt such intersection of God's time with our *chronos* and inner times that the kairotic event happens. When this occurs—the right time for the hearer—

we understand better what Luther meant by calling faith "an acoustical affair."

Fine: so why don't we do it? How is it that Buttrick's preacher on the passage in Luke "treats the passage as if it were a still-life picture in which some*thing* may be found, object-like, to preach on?" Why, if life is lived in time, would the preacher remove the central dynamic component?

Certainly Buttrick is correct that our academic background has helped create the problem. Our educational systems are geared to make truth stand still. In science we isolate variables until one stands alone—unconnected and lifeless. Thanks to Plato we pursue philosophic truth that ultimately resides in an essence so undynamic that one can speak of anything as participating in anythingness. Certainly the Hellenistic flavor of our educational life has had its impact, as has the fact that our language gives precedence to nouns— subjects and objects.

The central issue to our predicament is our focus on space as contrasted to time (as we discussed in the first chapter). We like to deal with *matters* that we can handle. Time, however, is so elusive. Uncomfortable with this state of affairs, we spatialize it; as Henri Bergson would say, "convert it into separate, distinct, measurable quantities which always remain separate, disparate, and unrelated, like points in space or marks on a chronometer."

So we head to the Sunday morning worship service and sing about the "unmoved mover" who created the universe. Yet, make no mistake about it, there is no unmoved mover in the Old Testament, where the names of the Deity are drawn from verbs: ruling, shepherding, judging, saving. And God "walks in the garden in the cool of the day" (Gen. 3 : 8). The *action* of creation, the time of it, the process of it, the resultant temporality—the event-in-time is the central dynamic. Even the term *"Kingdom,"* explains Crossan, "designates for us primarily a place or region; it includes subjects and, potentially, a king. But the primary emphasis of the original

36

Semitic term was not a *place*, but the *act* of God in which kingly rule and dominion was clearly manifested."[11]

Hence, we who dare to preach must enter the realm of time. To be faithful to the event-in-time called creation, to be true to the acoustical nature of faith, to prompt the kairotic moment of revelation means that we had better begin doing time in the pulpit. And perhaps the most powerful vehicle in doing so—at least in the context of our concerns here— is *story*, yet still another kind of time.

So, "once upon a time is a signal to pay attention to a discrete moment in time which can give meaning to all of time."[12]

"One day back when I was a kid on the farm . . . "

"A man once gave a great banquet . . . "

"When shall we meet again, in thunder, lightning, or in rain . . . ?"

"In the day that the Lord God made the earth. . . ."

The story begins, and we know, as the authors remind us, that it is "time to lean forward, to enter in, to let ourselves be moved along."[13] Stories involve time—fictional time, mythic time, historical time—any time will do. The moment we know that *time* is involved we attend. Stories as read, heard, seen on stage and screen involve their own time. Sometimes the characters of a book will live through several years in our single sitting. Or a rather lengthy play may involve only a few minutes of story time. A sermon may retell the good Samaritan story, and we relive *story time* at the pleasure— and we hope good timing—of the preacher. Time *inside* the story is *story time*.

Among many other time classifications that could be included,[14] there remains one more for our consideration— briefly now, and with considerable reflection later. This time I call *narrative time*.

When the storyteller stands up to a crowd, when the novelist frames the beginning lines, when the filmmaker reveals the opening scene, and when the preacher looks up from the pulpit toward the people for sermon time, *narrative time* begins. Picking up *chronos* and *inner*, reaching for *story*, announcing *God's* and praying for *kairos*, narrative time dances in, through, and around all the times. In one sense measurable by *chronos* but never overcome by it, and intending to transform it, narrative time *is* the play, *is* the novel, *is* the sermon. More later.

But note: this focus on story as the vehicle of temporality and time as oral mode must not be reduced to some kind of commitment to anecdotal style. We are not dealing here with how to insert an occasional illustration or passing anecdote to lift the eyelids. We are considering the sermon as an ordered form of moving time. To understand what is involved in such a definition of preaching one needs to examine *"story"*—its elements, its magic, and its time. To this crucial task we now turn.

Chapter Three

THE STORY'S TIME

"For we dream in narrative, daydream in narrative, remember, anticipate, hope, despair, believe, doubt, plan, revise, criticize, construct, gossip, learn, hate and love by narrative," says Barbara Hardy. "In order really to live, we make up stories about ourselves and others, about the personal as well as the social past and future."[1]

The powerful purpose of every story ever told—in one sense or another—is to order life meaningfully. Says Wicker: "The story gives a coherent shape to what would otherwise be a jumble of miscellanous, unintelligible items." Or as Stephen Crites would suggest: "Consciousness is created by story, and not story by consciousness."[2]

Little wonder then that a child when facing the dissolution called sleep will plead: "Tell me a story." Before we complain that the request is a delaying tactic, we may need to consider that one *must* delay until reassured of identity as a real member of the human race. Once, when very young, my daughter Jill was slipping off to sleep more quickly than my arrival for our good-night kiss. Dreams were almost in her eyes when she looked up and with magnificent abandon said: "I'm pretending to be a melting icecube." To be willing to "melt" one must be able to trust that somehow all is well. Tell me a story. Thinking of the Kalahari Bush people, Laurens Van Der Post said: "These people know what we do not: that without a story you have not got a nation, or a culture, or a civilization. Without a story of your own to live you haven't got a life of your own."[3] Please, tell me a story!

In a story form the Scriptures commence: "In the beginning God created the heavens and the earth" (Gen. 1:1), and still in story form the Scriptures conclude: "Then I saw a new heaven and a new earth" (Rev.21:1). Moreover: "The impact of a story" as explained by Lonnie D. Kliever "is not limited to the life exemplified or the principle illustrated in the story. Stories have the power to shape life because they formally embody the shape of life."[4]

"I am the Alpha and the Omega, the beginning and the end" (Rev.21:6), while we are in the middle—hearing and rehearing the Story in countless forms. Strangely it is not just about ancient characters and events, as Amos Wilder notes; rather, "they are always about us. They locate us in the very midst of the great story and plot of all time and space, and therefore relate us to the great dramatist and storyteller, God himself."[5] As Craddock would articulate it, the narrative "locates" us as "participants in time and place" and "reassures us that we are alive."

Hence every culture, religious tradition, nation, lodge, or community, of whatever sort, has its stories, which maintain its identity. Whether an ancient folktale for the sake of amusement or a sacred myth to justify the group's existence, the story-line becomes the life-line of the group. Of course the community is greater than the story, but because that greater reality is indefinable—a mysterious "more"—and because that mysterious more is evoked only by story, the narrative's power is in fact increased.

Explains Crites: "These stories seem to be allusive expressions of stories that cannot be fully and directly told, because they live, so to speak, in the . . . celebrants."[6] Similarly, Henry Mitchell identifies the "transconscious" quality of black preaching that reaches the "level of communally stored wisdom and cultural affinity."[7]

So we are "swept along" says Carl Jung, on a "subterranean current." And as L'Engle notes: "Long before Jung came up with his theories of archetypical understanding, William James wrote: 'Our lives are like islands in the sea, or like trees in the forest, which co-mingle their roots in the darkness underground.' "

All of this I shall understand more powerfully in two weeks, when our family endures a three-hundred-mile car trip to the Lowry family reunion. Although an annual affair, we make it about every other year—and part of me wonders why at all. Most of my relatives there will be people I hardly know—and who probably wouldn't call me on the phone if they were to pass through the town where I live. "Oh, so you are Homer's grand-niece; I see." But these strangers are different; we are family. And the call to roots is essentially a call to story. I am traveling to who I am. We will catch up on the events of those we know and will hear the old stories again—how Great Uncle Fred used to have a rubber hose reaching from his bed to outside his bedroom window—wanted fresh air handy! And I will by reconstituted again, set into the stream of time with a name once more. It is, after all, not a family re-collection, or even a family re-gathering; it is a family *reunion*.

Every time we go to church it is at the very least a trip to a family reunion, and at best it is a homecoming. Because Abraham and Sarah are also my family—and yours. Mary and Martha, James and John too. To hear their stories is to hear our story. We—all of us—are reconstituted again, set into the stream of time with a name once more.

So the fundamentalist preacher tells the trite story about the sinner and his wickedness—but who accepted Jesus just before he died (or who didn't). Present are those who hear their lives being recounted, and walk the aisle others had walked before (some of those others may now in their seats be walking it again). Or the priest elevates the host and tells a story: "On the night in which he was betrayed Jesus took the bread . . ." and they all receive it again. The rabbi is reading the list of names he read a year ago—except a few more have been added. It is the list of those faithful ones now taken in death and whose life*times* are marked on this particular

Sabbath for all the community to remember. Meanwhile many mainline Protestant congregations are hearing *ideas* from the pulpit—good ideas, well-organized, you understand—but ideas without the animation of story's time. And the people hunger for something with life in it, something with which they can identify or relive. Even a familiar "old" hymn before the sermon could help them recall the time when Granddad was alive and present in the service. But the hymn "isn't good music; too subjective," and is not chosen for use. But most important, the story—where is the recreating story? "How could it have happened," asks L'Engle, "that even in the church *story* has been lost as a vehicle of truth?"

Answers Roth: "The vitality of the original stories was lost because in their pious earnestness to convey the message or grasp the goal men forgot to tell the tale," In one sense it is a natural sequence: "First came the religious vision, then the aesthetic expression of it, then the ethical emulation of it, and finally the philosophical rationalization as explanation and apology." But he concludes: "My contention is that the story itself is reality."[8]

Roth is joined in that conclusion by the never-ending procession of narrative artists of many persuasions through the ages. Jean-Paul Sartre, for example, sees the purpose of literature to "restore to the event its brutal freshness, its ambiguity, its unforeseeability." "To put it boldly," says Kort, "narratives create their own power and meaning; they create author and reader just as author and reader create them. They do this by having certain properties with which the author and the reader, like it or not, have to cope." To which we ask: What certain powerful properties? We all should like to know! As preachers we need to know.

Kort's answer is that the power of story emerges "because of and in terms of its elements," which are "setting, plot, character, and tone." Hence, we are going to explore the interactions of these four elements—plus a fifth element that I will add. First, however, we need to clarify some terms. Kort speaks of author and reader, but before that there were teller and listener. Scholes and Kellogg in their definitive work, *The Nature of Narrative*, explain that every literary narrative work has two characteristics: "the presence of a story and a story teller." They use the term literary or literature in the broad sense of "all verbal art, both oral and written."

Drama or the dramatic arts, they maintain, is distinguished from narrative in the fact that a drama has "a story without a story teller." This certainly seems a clear distinction until they try to make a case for film being narrative rather than dramatic in form. They contend that because of the "controlled point of view, the eye of the camera," its distance and focus, the fact of music, sound effects, and so on, that film "does not present a story directly, without narration." But if control is the key then why not call drama a form of narrative too? Although using different technologies the playwright and actors also *control our view* by providing a very selective slice of the potential fictional world for us to experience. Hence in definition I include both drama and film as forms of narrative art.

When a person forms a story, or tells another's story, the elements of setting, character, action, plot, and tone, and their interactions provide the story's mix. Every preacher who stands up to retell a parable of Jesus, or recount a biblical event, or frame a contemporary story must cooperate, utilize, and be influenced by these definable elements. Although we properly are warned not to "assert in an a priori way that one of the elements of narrative always will be dominant,"[9] yet the elements will receive unequal treatment in this writing—primarily because of our concern for the issue of time, and partly as an outgrowth of my own convictions.

Setting

The story must be located in space and time—however natural or fantastic or, obviously, it is no story. In large measure story, by its very form, overcomes one quite important problem otherwise encountered in verbal address, namely the problem of abstract-concrete polarity. How often we have been admonished to be specific or be concrete in our preaching. Abstractions, abstractions—we have advanced degrees in them. Yet the reverse problem is just as frustrating—as when the children insist on telling detail after detail of last night's episode of their favorite television show: "He did this, and she did that, and. . . ." But not having experienced the story ourselves, we cannot get the picture. So Wendell Johnson, in *People in Quandaries*, utilized Korzybski's "abstraction ladder" concept and advises any communicator to go up and down the ladder—that is, present the particularity of eggs *and* also provide baskets to put them in. But note how in a story located in space and time the polarities of abstract/concrete and general/specific are overcome. The story moves through inner and outer action, development of character, and progression of plot—and by so doing, the extremes of abstract and concrete are merged into event. In a specific moment of action the listeners make their own paradigmatic abstractions, and conversely a general concept is presented before our very ears in event. And the form story takes transcends such polarities with power because that's the way we actually live our own lives.

The importance of setting in a story, however, is not simply that life is *located*, but that life is *limited*. Setting produces the objectivity of otherness, those conditions of time, place, and circumstance that Kort says "the characters or narrator cannot change." Nor, for that matter, can we the listeners or readers. Compare telling a congregation about "this woman, a college friend of mine, who just before her last year of school had this horrendously difficult vocational decision to make . . . " with urging the congregation to "recognize that it is of the nature of human existence to be finite."

In more than one sense, finitude is a most difficult concept to grasp—if one is forced to do so—but the woman's impending decision is close to home. We all understand. Plus the fact that through story you "overhear" your own finitude, as Craddock would say, by means of "indirection."[10] When we listen to a story we think we are attending to some fictional life out there; we are swept into the plot without our defenses up. Then we discover it is *our* life that is being displayed and addressed—but alas it is too late to prevent hearing.

Moreover, in modern fiction, "characters find themselves in worlds which tend not to grant them what they need and desire."[11] Sound like your congregation? It is within the given imposition of what Kort calls "negative atmosphere" that characters make their moves and incidents evolve into plot. And when a parishioner slaps you on the back with the familiar words: "Well, preacher, I guess you'll never be out of a job," what is being conveyed (at least in part) is that all of us are set into just such a world. "The comedy of grace," as Buechner evokes it, "as what needn't happen and can't possibly happen because it can only impossibly happen and happens in the dark that only just barely fails to swallow it up."[12] That's our world all right—and the very reason Buechner in his Lyman Beecher Lectures began with the inevitability of the *tragic* first, before moving on to the unforeseeability of the *comic*.

So the stage of the story is set with both explicit and implicit borders. Robert Frost lets us see both kinds of borders in the closing lines of "Stopping by Woods on a Snowy Evening" by the simple repetition of a single line, which the second time through shifts meaning altogether:

> The woods are lovely, dark, and deep
> But I have promises to keep
> And miles to go before I sleep
> And miles to go before I sleep.[13]

These borders shortly will press in closer and closer by means of the circumstances of events and the decisions of characters.

There is a special reason why the borders of setting as naturally provided by story are crucial to people of our profession. We are by definition "answer people." Everybody knows the gospel means *solution*. Our congregations would be not only surprised but angered if we concluded the sermon with anything like: "So we too are waiting for Godot, or night to fall." This just will not do. And although we complain about people who always expect quick answers from us—in the pulpit and out—yet we have learned to expect this expectation and to respond. In fact, on occasion there is some measure of pleasure to it. So we waltz in where angels fear to tread, Bible in hand and false confidence on our face. (I suspect physicians and a few lawyers know what I mean.)

Translated into pulpit work, we often announce the gospel's successful resolution even before we have adequately identified the angst of the problem. Even our sermon titles, displayed on the bulletin board outside or in mimeographed bulletins inside, suggest happy resolution: "Fortunate Misfortune" or "Christian Victory" or "Prayer as Power" or "The Triumphant Adequacy of Christ."[14]

The consequence is worse than letting the homiletical cat out of the bag. It suggests, at least to the more thoughtful, that in fact we may not take the borders of existence seriously. So when we conclude triumphantly, "I can do all things through Christ," some wonder just how real is the victory. (In all fairness this is not our problem alone. James L. Adams, addressing the question of creative problem-solving in *Conceptual Blockbusting*, laments that in all kinds of fields of problem-solving endeavor "problem statements are often liberally laced with answers,"[15] which of course forecloses the possibility of a more creative solution.)

But if the sermonic form is story, there is little way we can duck the borders of existence because the negative atmosphere of setting will of necessity provide them. One could hardly retell the prodigal son story beginning with the homecoming and omitting the pig pen. The question is not whether a sermon will conclude with: "I can do all things"; the question is whether the moment of arriving at this miracle of grace is made credible by the process of confronting formidable obstacles. The very form of story facilitates this credibility.

The element of setting, then, is a particularly powerful and important ingredient—a gift from the narrative arts to us who preach. Fortunately the "negative atmosphere" of setting is not the only element in narrative. As objective otherness, setting is engaged in battle by the subjectivities of character.

Character

Into the story walks the character, or a whole cast. The woman caught in adultery, or Zacchaeus up in the tree, or Joseph's brothers coming for help, or Ruth arriving in a new homeland, or Willy Loman, briefcase in hand, or the college classmate facing the vocational decision. Character in narrative "is an image primarily of the potential of human consciousness to know and manage the world in which it finds itself."[16] But we need to be careful with that term "potential." (Surely we need not be limited to the assumptions of the "human potential" movement to use it.) Here we mean simply that whatever powers of decision, growth, accomplishment, even sacrifice are available, they are going to be summoned by the story. (The assumed definition of human nature or condition as any particular narrator understands it is a part of what is meant by the narrative element of "tone"—to be considered later.) Such potential is not announced point blank; it is lived out through the plot of the story. And the point of it all is not *announced definition* but *lived conflict*—the given objectivities being faced in battle by the inner subjectivities of the characters. Of course the battle does not stay pure—simply the objectivity of setting against the subjectivity of the character (one negative; one positive). For the characters also do battle among and within themselves. Sometimes the enemy called setting is only a hint of the real enemy inside.

At long last the power of character in narrative, according to Kort, is due to the resultant "paradigms that illuminate the human potential for good and evil." *"Paradigms that illuminate?"* What precisely is meant by such a phrase as that?

The best way I know to get at it is to notice another peculiarity of people—one rather crisply perceived among clergy. In spite of Browne's warning that "because the ineffable remains the ineffable," and that therefore the best we can do is "to make gestures toward it,"[17] *we yet want to nail it down.* Gestures are so inadequately tentative. So, often we *do* nail it down.

Ask us what we think about human nature and we will tell you: "People can do whatever they really choose to do. It is a matter of the will." Or: "People are caught in the web of circumstance, and will do whatever the situation demands." Seldom is this breezy summation of humanness convincing to others. Worse yet, we ourselves are not really convinced—at least not at a deeper level. So we seldom really behave according to our "principles" and "definitions." Hypocrisy? Not necessarily. We simply may be behaving appropriately. Have you ever noticed how our doctrine of human nature shifts when we move from pulpit to counseling chamber? Each field demands a definition, and each gets one. Often they don't happen to match, and we vacillate between two views, neither of which we really believe fully. When the traveler asked the St. Louis cab driver to explain why he was violating his long-held straight-ticket voting past to vote for a particular candidate of the other political party, the cabbie replied that sometimes you have to "push [your] principles aside and do the right thing."[18]

When confronted by the intricacies of real events as people actually experience them in time, our pat and precise definitions do not work. And most of us know all of this quite well in our usual rounds of ministry. But get us in the pulpit, and all of a sudden life turns simple, clear, and unambiguous! Browne offers an important corrective: "To speak the truth" is to "show the way to think and not to offer the results of thought; it is to sharpen . . . perception," not to "tell . . . what to see."

Now what *character* in narrative has the peculiar power to do is to sharpen perception about *how* to think. By moving through the tale we get in touch with live realities in action, not the corpse of doctrinaire conclusions. The incidents, decisions, inner thoughts, and outer events of the plot get compressed into a gestaltive illumination. We are presented a conscious paradigm, perhaps to match the unconscious image we already know, but did not know that we knew. Or we are grasped by a new vision of life we never understood before. And that is what is meant by being provided with "paradigms that illuminate the human potential."

Buechner told me he never knew beforehand that Leo Bebb was going to turn out the hero in *Lion Country*—let alone that when he finished writing the book, three more books would follow—"because the story wasn't through with me." And has not a similar experience been yours? You begin sermon preparation on an Old Testament narrative. You already know what you're going to say—sort of. But then the passage begins leading you down a new road. Perhaps you are paraphrasing a scene out loud to yourself, and then you begin saying things and seeing things you'd never thought before. You are utterly surprised with it all and suddenly, being grasped by this illumination of the paradigm of character, your new homiletical question is: How can I relive this experience in the pulpit in such a way that they can see and hear what I just saw and heard?

So at long last and through the means of identification, the most important character in the narrative becomes oneself. I am the one finally discovered. At the theater, in the novel, and within the text I find *me* as I never knew me before. All this is possible because through characterization as lived out in incident/action/plot, hard-to-define aspects of human existence are revealed for the world to behold. Character in narrative, however, and in spite of the gestalt-like illumination, is never a timeless snapshot of reality. It is very much alive and moving, because character is set in the thread of action.

Action

When I spoke with Frederick Buechner on the telephone to arrange an interview and told him I was interested in what he could tell me about *plot*, he responded that he didn't know anything about it (indeed, it was the last thing to emerge in his writings). Of course I knew better because I had read several of his novels as well as his theological writings. But his demurrer was not a case of artistic modesty. It was that for him the term *plot* was something different than for me—a difference that is reflected in the literature on the subject. When I asked about *plot*, he took the question to refer to *action*. Many experts consider the two terms virtually interchangeable. I am choosing to distinguish between them. Since for me *plot* is the larger term, we need to define it now before we can press on to describe *action*.

What does the term "plot" mean? Or rather, what do we mean by the term? Here are several options:

> Muir: "The term plot. . .designates. . .the chain of events in a story and the principle which knits it together."
>
> Scholes and Kellogg: "Plot can be defined as the dynamic, sequential element in narrative literature."
>
> Aristotle: Plot is ". . .the energy, the action in time, and informing movement of ideas."
>
> Dipple: "Plot is the arrangement of action: action progresses through the indispensable medium of time from which it derives all of its modifying vocabularies."
>
> R. S. Crane: "Plot is a synthetic word and has three causal modifications, producing plots of action, plots of character, and plots of thought."

The question that emerges from the various definitions and that requires our attention is: Does the term *plot* refer to *incident, action,* or *chain of events only,* or is the term's referent to be taken as including some additional principle or movement not covered by the terms incident, action, or chain of events? When I asked Buechner about "plot" he took the former strand of definition while I assumed the latter. Later I was to learn that when he said plot was the last thing to happen, he meant that his method was to concentrate on character—to stay in the presence of the characters and essentially be alert to follow where they might lead. My concern was with strategies of story resolution, by which I mean an opening conflict that gains complication, does a strange turn, and finally is resolved. I take that to be the essential feature of plot. As best as I understand him, Buechner subsumes these essential attributes of story within character development.

Besides, at the deeper level professional narrative artists have so internalized the necessities of conflict/complication/reversal/denouement that it is scarcely identifiable any more. It becomes as much second nature to most of us as walking: shift weight/lift/ place/shift weight/lift/place. But for us whose background is homiletical rhetoric and not narrative art, these matters become crucial. If these concerns are left unattended, a few preachers will happen on to the gist of it while the rest of us are left wondering why it is that "some can do it and others can't." In order to facilitate our addressing these larger concerns of movement and resolution, we will limit our present consideration to the narrower focus of action, incident, or event—and then provide a new, separate section of *plot*.

Regarding *action*: It is difficult to imagine a narrative in which once the setting is provided (we know where we are and when) and the characters introduced (we learn their names at least) that nothing would happen except inner developing thoughts. Perhaps it is possible, but normally actions occur. External events transpire, impacting the lives of characters who must respond internally and externally, and whose responses in turn become the genesis of further action. Jesus is walking into and among the crowd, looks up at Zacchaeus in the tree, and invites him down. Zacchaeus promptly falls out of the tree, brushes himself off, and leads the way to his house. While they walk—presumably at a normal pace—Zacchaeus' thoughts are racing back and forth, while the thoughts of the crowd are doing a slow burn. The parade was a flop, but

Zacchaeus' future is new. Action, response, new action—on and on, relentless, new, old, strange, expected. Something always happens next.

Depending on the particular author's purpose and style, action may be dominant, resulting in an adventure story; character may be dominant, resulting in a character study. But either way *something else is going on.* I call this something else *plot.*

Plot

"All plots depend on tension and resolution," say Scholes and Kellogg simply, and we sense they are on the right track. But *plot* is not a separate entity from the tension and resolution; *it is their unified whole.* Plot *is* that movement about which we speak when we refer to tension and resolution. Hence I define plot as follows: *A plot is the moving suspense of story from disequilibrium to resolution.*

Viewing plot this way helps us to understand how it is that two stories that appear so different in form, because one concentrates on sequential action while the other concentrates on character development, have so much in common. Each represents a different kind of movement, *but both move.* Both are set in the context of a plot. Were we to define plot as the "arrangement of action" our definition would impel us to say that an adventure story narrative was strong on plot and the character development story was not. Such is not the case. The one uses character as the primary means, the other action. In both stories there is *something at stake.* The integrity of both stories hangs in the balance of successful resolution. And so does our interest. As Scholes and Kellogg put it: "The reader of a narrative can expect to finish his reading having achieved a state of equilibrium—something approaching calm of mind, all passion spent." When this state of equilibrium has not been reached the result is incompletion. Aristotle complained of such a result, labeling the underlying plot both as "episodic" in the sense of there being "no probability or necessity for the order" and as "the worst kind." In my judgment the otherwise entertaining and even stimulating movie *Four Seasons* failed in its bid for profound impact precisely here, that the four episodes lacked probability or necessity for the order and hence did not adequately provide resolution. Dealing with similar subject matter, *Ordinary People* was powerful. The critical difference, in my view, had to do with the form of the plot.

Moving suspense of story from disequilibrium to resolution is so basic, so deeply ingrained, so second-nature to professional narrative artists that scarcely do they have to think about it, sometimes they even have difficulty verbalizing about it, but it is the key to plot. Most of us preachers, however, come from another discipline and must learn of these things step by step. Later perhaps it can become second nature to us too.

Our act of defining the term *plot* should be a good starting point, but it is not as simple as it seems. For example, my choice of the term "disequilibrium" to identify the opening stage of a story has been most difficult. So many different terms are utilized by narrative theorists, and other terms plead for inclusion. The terms *discrepancy, conflict, ambiguity, tension, void*—all could be used, and each has a particular contribution to make. Sometimes I will even use the terms interchangeably. Yet, the selection of terminology itself raises several worthy issues. And by the words *moving suspense* do we mean objectively, that is, in the purpose of the author or narrator? Or subjectively, in the listener, reader, or observer? Or narratively, as in the story? Actually, I mean all three. The term *conflict* is particularly apt for conveying the objective sense of the author's intent. The story's creator has set a battle before us for a reason, and only when victory and defeat occur in the story can resolution be said to have occurred and the author's point made. Yet the term *conflict* is not always apt. Every preacher knows the result of inserting a sermonic illustration. "Once, when . . ." is all it takes for the eyes to refocus and pulses to quicken. You can hardly call this maneuver the introduction of conflict. Perhaps *tension* would express it, meaning the sense of disequilibrium on the part of the listener or reader. When you cannot lay a book down—even though you have other things you need to be doing—because you are experiencing an incompleteness, you feel the tension born of discrepancy. Yet the term tension as illustrated might seem to subjectivize the matter, as though the reader creates the plot by the act of reading.

Actually, both the artist in the creation of a story and the "receiver" of the narrative art form are making a statement about the world. Chaos needs ordering, and narrative art's purpose is to accomplish the deed. But there is another locus of void or ambiguity involved in narrative. Says T. S. Eliot: "The poem's existence is somewhere between the writer and the reader; it has a reality which is not simply the reality of what the writer is trying to express," and I would add: nor simply the function of the reader's nervous system.

This third sense as applied to moving suspense or ambiguity is as difficult to define as it is easy to experience: It is the bottom of the ninth; the score is 4 to 3, bases loaded, 2 outs, 3 balls—2 strikes on the batter, who connects with a line drive sharply hit deep into the right field corner—right on the foul line. The outfielder races to catch it, the runners speed toward the plate, and the umpire charges down the base line. The outfielder dives for the catch, right at ground level, and emerges with ball in glove. But did he catch it or trap it? Was it fair or foul? If the ball touched the ground inside the line the runner is on with two RBIs. Score 5 to 4—the batter's team wins. If the ball was trapped in foul territory the game's still on and the batter remains at the plate. If the ball was caught—fair or foul—it is three outs and the ball game—for the outfielder's team wins 4 to 3. Certainly there is subjective tension, felt in the stadium's silence. And there is objective reality. Either the ball was in fact caught, or was trapped. It was in or out. Perhaps the instant replay will tell us, but without effect on the game. The *real* reality has not yet happened—not until the official's word: *out*, or *fair ball*, or *foul ball.* In a similar way the story has its own word, separate from the objectivity of the author's intent or the subjectivity of the reader's feeling. When writers say: "I listen to the story" or "I listen to the characters," they bear witness to their active waiting for the official's call. One reason a story grips us so as we read is that we are not the only ones waiting for a void to be filled or an ambiguity to be resolved. The author, too, while writing—performing the role of "midwife" as Eliseo Vivas phrased it[19]—is waiting for the birth of order to supplant chaos. The moving suspense from disequilibrium to resolution is the very heart of story, the principle of its form, and the genius of its power.

Moreover, we feel it in our bones. Steven Crites notes how ingeniously Frank Kermode has created

> "tick-tock" as a model of plot, contrasting the organized duration between the "humble genesis" of tick and the "feeble apocalypse" of tock with the emptiness, the unorganized blank that exists between our perception of "tock" and the next "tick" [So the characters exist] between the tick of "once upon a time" and the tock of happy resolution.[20]

When I first heard of Kermode's metaphor I thought perhaps humor had outdistanced the conveyed point, but the more I mused the more convinced I became of its profundity. Just ask anyone to repeat slowly the words "tick-tock" and notice the voice inflection. Tick goes up into suspense; tock comes down in resolution. Also the sound of tick involving a frontal vowel leaves you hanging up in the air; tock involving a middle vowel sets you down. And have you ever tried to reverse the tick and tock of a grandfather clock once you have established which was which? Only with great difficulty. Indeed, the metaphor evokes exactly what I mean by the suspense, the ambiguity with which a plot begins.

Before moving on to the next stage in the journey of plot, I want to note what I do *not* mean by the term *ambiguity*. This term as a noun expresses well the suspense created by story. Somehow, by a strange function of language usage, when the term is placed in adjectival form, that is: *ambiguous*, the denotation seems to shift (and dictionaries reflect the shift by reversing the primary meanings). In my use here I do *not* mean ambiguity or ambiguous in the sense of *imprecision*, but ambiguity—the *not-yet-known* quality born of expectation. This is a difference of great importance to the preacher; hence, I will discuss it more fully in the next chapter, "Narrative Time."

So the story's suspense begins with disequilibrium, ambiguity, tension, or conflict. Perhaps it need not evidence a stronger dosage of suspense than mere *incompleteness*. We all require large amounts of closure—windows closed and doors shut. But then your spouse arrives home from work and says: "Strange thing happened in the car just now . . . ," or a friend walks up and asks: "Have you heard the one about . . . ?" Or, your child enters the room in the middle of your conversation and demands everyone restart at the beginning. The arresting power of even a little incompletion launches a whole fictional world, and breathlessly we follow where it leads. Narrative artists touch the nerve of human life here. So did the serpent as it turned to the woman with: "Did God really say that . . . ?" (Gen. 3:2, paraphrase). All this is possible not by means of cheap manipulative cleverness but by touching us at the very center of human finitude. We will not rest until the matter finds closure. In its most radical formulation: "Restless, is our heart until it comes to rest in thee" (Augustine). The trouble is, the ultimate resolution as we Christians understand it is Christ Jesus—and the surprise of this revelation is that instead of matters ending here, things have only just begun. Says Browne: "Religion is not a way of mastering . . . complexity, but of bearing it."

The typical plot begins with perhaps only a touch of disequilibrium—or perhaps with an important opening conflict—but then "allows" things to get worse. No matter what the source of the suspense, whether a detective trying to solve a crime or a couple trying to work through marital conflict, somehow far beyond midpoint of the story, everyone—

character, author, reader—is further away from solution than when it all began. Decisions made by the characters that by all odds should have resulted in progress have in fact caused regression. Circumstances as occurring through incident have complicated things further. Opening disequilibrium has escalated into heightened ambiguity. The situation is utterly irresolute—or so it seems.

But then a strange corner is turned. The thing that could not possibly happen, does, and the obvious eventuality does not. The villain places the final stone in his impenetrable castle of oppression—secure now forever—and the building falls into a thousand pieces. The bungling researcher whose proven incompetence has thwarted everyone else's work for so long that now we come to expect it, arrives at the office of the departmental head for dismissal and stumbles onto the solution while tripping through the office doorway. Aristotle utilized the term "peripety" to define it, and explains that it is "a shift of what is being undertaken to the opposite in the way previously stated, and that in accordance with probability or necessity." So for example: "In the *Oedipus*, the man who has come, thinking that he will reassure Oedipus, that is, relieve him of his fear with respect to his mother, by revealing who he once was, brings about the opposite; and in the *Lynceus*, as he (Lynceus) is being led away with every prospect of being executed, and Danaus pursuing him with every prospect of doing the executing, it comes about as a result of the other things that have happened in the play that *he* is executed and Lynceus is saved."

John Dominic Crossan explains the radicality of reversal as found in the parables of Jesus—not just single or double reversals, but "polar reversals."He explains that "Where the north pole becomes the south pole, and the south the north, a world is reversed and overturned, and we find ourselves standing firmly on utter uncertainty . . . Such is the advent of the Kingdom." The last becomes the first and the first becomes last.

Once things are turned upside-down (an event generally occurring well toward the end of the story), the tale winds down into completion—into resolution. The term often used for this closing stage is *denouement*, which means literally, *unraveling*. But the term does not denote the coming apart of the story or plot; if it did the tension would increase. Rather it means that closure born of the unexpected, the surprising turn now reshapes both character and event, and we are given a short glimpse of the future as it is now newly given. Denouement—and what has unraveled, is the moving suspense. A totally new equilibrium emerges, and the tale is told.

Plot: the moving suspense of story, from disequilibrium to resolution. Its typical stages are (1) opening disequilibrium, gaining complication toward (2) escalated ambiguity, climaxing into (3) reversal, and moving out into (4) denouement. This is the plot of a typical story as a narrator tells it and surely the shape of a sermon, which orders experience as a preacher proclaims it.

But does this mean what it appears to suggest—that every preacher must become a novelist and every sermon begin with words equivalent to "once upon a time"? By no means, although Jesus did indeed teach almost exclusively through the medium of story. Our purpose here is to learn what narrative art can teach us, and the *shape* of story's plot is perhaps the most important lesson we can learn—the ramifications of which we will indeed explore (in the next chapter). First, though, we need to complete our brief look at the elements of story, (setting, character, action, plot, and tone) and quickly identify the impact of time upon story.

Tone

"The novels are too religious for the secular," reflected Buechner on his own writing, "and too secular for the religious."[21] In making such a remark Buechner was addressing the narrative element of *tone.* Perhaps for some the term *tone* is misleading because they infer that some kind of superficial quality is being discussed. That is not at all what Kort means by the term. Rather, *tone* refers to the work's *created subjective presence*—the world view that stands silently articulate behind the writing. What Buechner was addressing is not simply what is actually written (which is perhaps the smaller part of the matter) but the convictions *behind* what is written—even what is excluded. Some writers prefer *point of view* to the term *tone*.[22]

The often-heard phrase about where someone "is coming from" says it exactly, and *where* a narrative artist is coming from exerts an enormous silent control over the story. It shapes the handling of character, the sequence of action, the suspense of plot. When a few pages back I complained about plotless stories that run through episodes with little resolution, I was doing more than identifying what the term "plot" means. There was a silent norm about story I was living out in my writing. I could have been merely descriptive—indicating that some stories are episodic while others have plot. But my implied preference "comes from" a basic conviction about human existence. If our lives are not microcosmic of the larger plot of history—and God's creation—and hence if stories do not reflect this plot-like nature of existence, then as a Christian preacher—even as a human being—I have nothing to say nor anything to hear. For me, plot form is ontologically superior to episodic form. It's just that simple.

I mentioned to Buechner that a lot of us were taught in seminary preaching classes not to use anecdotes out of our own lives—nor for that matter, really to consider our own history when dealing with the Word. I started to say that such a viewpoint seemed to me to be . . . and he finished my sentence with a single word: "Nuts!" Later he explained: "It seems to me that the word we preach is an incarnate word; it's the center of our faith. And this is true not only in terms of the Logos Word, the word made flesh in Christ, but the words that God speaks to us through the events of our own lives, and if you don't talk about those words—if you don't deal with the flesh and blood events of your own and your congregation's lives—then most of what you say will be dim and irrelevant."[23]

Our conversation, you see, was focused on *tone*, dealing with assumptions and convictions that automatically inform our work. I recall from seminary days the academic reaction to anything subjective. Funeral meditations, for example, must not be subjective eulogies, but proclamations of the Promise. I took the advice to mean "not personal," and for several years beyond seminary prided myself on being able to get through a funeral without mentioning the name of the deceased.

How we deal with subject matter in a sermon often says more than *what* we say about it. So Helmut Thielicke concludes that "the trouble with the church" can be traced to the pulpit utterances of those who believe what they say—but unfortunately what they say does not come from the vital center of their lives.[24] Somehow the reality of tone comes through. So, too, the preacher who is trying so hard to address openly and descriptively a current controversial issue or sticky ethical question may instead reveal a contrary, even judgmental tone, just by style and nuance.

Tone also has to do with *point of view* in the technical narrative sense discussed earlier—whether the viewpoint is that of character, narrator, audience, author, or preacher. By means of redaction criticism, often we can make distinctions in a biblical text—where, for example, the genuine parable of Jesus leaves off and the editor's additions begin. But not only did the writer of Mark utilize Jesus' words to make the writer's point, and Luke, then, alter it to make his, we then alter it further to fit ours—only this latter stage is not so easily discernible, human nature being what it is. Indeed, there is some considerable pleasure in watching a Pauline preacher dance in, around, and through Matthew's account called the Sermon on the Mount. *Power* is the point, *control* the means, *tone* the result.

Put them all together—setting, character, action, plot, and tone—and you have the peculiar elements of story. Impacting them all is the facticity of time running like a current through them and carrying them on their way. Of course all the elements involve story space as well—*but they exist in time. Time* is the necessary medium. Not only is this true in the sense that the story is literally bracketed within a time-frame—the story time in which characters move from one time to another—but also true in the sense of the author's extraordinary dependence upon the vehicle of time.

A narrative writer or speaker has great flexibility in the choice of incidents and localities (space). *This* doesn't have to happen, *that place* could be replaced. But a narrative writer or speaker cannot replace time. Time can be shuffled, such as by the technique of flashback; it can be stretched and compressed, as when a preacher retells a parable—elaborating here and speeding by there. But the givenness of time becomes the great restrictor and the great facilitator of story. *It is temporality*—and as such, story's closest link to you and me. We, too, can choose to be here or there, reflect on this or that, move forward or draw back, but we cannot choose to skip today and remain alive.

Then, finally, time is central because it takes *us* time to hear the sermon, attend the play, read the book. This I call narrative time.

Chapter Four

NARRATIVE TIME

It is 8:10 P.M., central daylight *chronos* time, August 6, in the Year of our Lord 1981. The curtain opens and the play begins. The playwright in his or her own good time has created the play with a fictional setting of Chicago. Between 8:10 and 10:43 P.M., *chronos* time, the audience will experience eighteen months of *story time* (March 1973 to Fall of 1974) in the fictional lives of the play's characters. Eighteen months of story time will be compressed into approximately two and one half hours of *narrative time*.

Meanwhile the would-be participants of this evening's event, the audience, have brought their various internal clocks with them—*inner times*, if you please—which will also take part in tonight's happening. For one, time is rushing and she can hardly slow things down enough to participate. On the other hand, inner time is hanging heavy for another, and he can scarcely get in gear for tonight's trip. And for all present, a passive willfulness must occur for the play to happen for them. It is not so much an active intention as it is a ceasing of resistance.

Once inside story time, all find their various times to be blending, contrasting, engaging in counterpoint with story time, as narrative time begins to supplant the rest. Fictional events, incidents, action in Chicago are happening on stage, while historical events in El Paso (1949), Cleveland (1973), and Madison (1980) are *recurring* in the audience—in some cases actually being re-formed into fresh, new experiences. Again, on stage conflict is building toward a climactic and unexpected turn, then moving out in denouement—not only experienced as story time in Chicago, summer of 1974, but strangely, Madison in late 1980, and a fresh, new 1973 in Cleveland. *Kairos time* moments are happening within the hall secretly, sometimes shared with another by the squeeze of a hand, as tonight's narrative time draws on story time on one side and the various times of the people on the other side—melting together into a new event-in-time. And this new event may even prompt a paradigmatic revelation for some, which as *God's time* will forever alter their times. Meanwhile, another member of the audience presses the illumination button on his digital wristwatch, and it is clear that for him time stands still in more ways than one.

By 10:43 P.M. the play is over, and among the many events that have happened, one thing is certain: the curtain has closed on an aesthetic event (not, mind you, an aesthetic object—for objects exist in space—but an event-in-time). Transcending this time for the purpose of reflection we note that what has happened objectively is first of all an occurrence of *narrative time*. This narrative time is the creation of the playwright, director, and the cast, and can be measured by *chronos* time: 8:10–10:43 P.M. (Last night the narrative time was three and a half minutes longer.)

From our point of view the earth has moved; we would say the sun has set. The baby-sitter will help us calculate the elapsed *chronos* which—there at the house—turned out to be a long inner time. But to the degree that during the play we were conscious of the passage of *chronos* time, to that degree we missed narrative time. Narrative time, then, is the meeting of story time brought by the playwright and various inner times, brought by the members of the audience, such as when—strangely like the Eucharist—our times are offered, blessed, fractured, and returned new.

Sermon time is another form of narrative time—measurable by the clock on the wall—and powerful, in one sense to the degree that nobody looked at that clock on the wall. We are the playwright, the director, and the cast, regardless of how we may choose to shape it. Our purpose is to take the times of our congregation and by means of story time hope to prompt a kairos time. Perhaps it will—we pray it might—become an occasion when God's time breaks into human history.

The Sermon as a Form of Narrative Time

At first this may perhaps seem an awesome way to think of our task, but whenever we step behind a pulpit this is indeed what is happening—like it or not. Actually, to conceive of sermon time as narrative time, bringing The Story into relationship with the congregation's various times, is to clarify what we are doing, and finally to make it simpler than before. True, in considering our task we will be using a few new terms and norms, but we will also be discarding some "old" terms and rules that are not, in my view, very helpful. Our task now is to see what a sermon shape looks like when imaged as narrative time.

Immediately we discover that to look at the definition of a plot, the underlying form of a story, is actually to view the shape of any sermon. If a plot is the *moving suspense of story—from disequilibrium to resolution*—then so is a sermon viewed from the perspective of narrative time. Any given sermon takes the form of moving suspense. This shape will have the same stages as the typical plot: opening disequilibrium, escalating into sharp ambiguity, until a surprising turn or reversal turns things around and allows the sermon to flow into denouement. But before we examine more precisely that swelling of tension and final release, we need to observe a couple of characteristics of suspense.

There are at least two sides to the coin of suspense. Suspense in story, in sermon, requires (to put it formally) both *objective* and *subjective* credibility. That is, first of all the source of the suspense must be "real" and must be viewed as such. We are dealing with the issue of there being *something at stake*, and it must be sensed as such by the listeners.

At this point I am unwilling to be sidetracked too far in asking what is "objective" and what is "subjective." With condescension we remember the question of how many angels can stand on the head of a pin—but we entertain our "superior" stance only because we are so certain that nothing in fact is at stake. If we could imagine what ultimate theological consequences were at stake behind the question, we might really get exercised about it—but we can't, so we won't. In a court of law a case may be dismissed as "frivolous"—meaning that in the opinion of the judge there is nothing significant at stake—and hence the case is a nuisance, becomes an affront to the dignity of the court, and is thrown out. Every congregation acts as judge here, and matters considered "frivolous," and hence not worth the engagement of mind and time, will be dismissed. And whether this conclusion is based on "objectivity" is beside the point. The decision is made.

I believe every sermon moves from an *itch* to a *scratch*—and the point here is that it must be the congregation's itch, not just mine as preacher. Yet the moment I make this last statement I recognize that apparently I am in theological trouble—at least with my own theological convictions (perhaps yours). Do I mean that the preacher is limited in the pulpit to those matters that *appear* to the congregation to be important? If so, then the preacher had better be prepared both to be greatly limited in selection of issues *and* also to entertain a very optimistic view of human nature. Have we so soon forgotten Barth's reminder that we go to the Bible with our questions only to have the Bible retort: "Nein, wrong question!" Not at all, nor should we forget the power of narrative art to place us, literally by a pull of the curtain, to places and times and issues we never once intended when we paid our money at the door. (Later in this chapter we will turn to Craddock's important contribution at this point by means of his concept of "overhearing the gospel" and how that relates to story.) For the time being, I think it enough to note that it is the congregation's passive willfulness that permits us to preach at all with anybody listening. Hence very quickly into the sermon the listeners' consent is utterly required. And the primary basis on which a positive assent is given is whether in their view *something is at stake*.

Beyond the "objective" issue of the something at stake, is the "subjective" side that bears on the relation between preacher and congregation. Leading any congregation through the phases and movement of suspense regarding any "real" issue requires the congregation's *trust*. That is, the listeners knowing we are about to lead them down a risky road—hopefully to some resolution born of the gospel—must have the confidence that we are capable of doing the job credibly, convincingly, theologically, and hopefully. This trust is a gift of the listeners and without it little can be accomplished in the pulpit.

Moreover, this trust is not just a matter of withholding judgment, of waiting to discover if they are going to agree with the preacher's conclusions. If there is significant preliminary doubt, they simply will not walk the road that will lead to *any* conclusion. Remember the problem we had watching the high school play? It was so difficult to be willing to accept the next-door teenager as Macbeth. Or again, recall the preview showing of the "religious drama" (copies available at the denominational bookstore). It certainly had a Christian message—except that it was thoroughly unreal. Just a short way into the first scene we knew the problem of credibility and wondered why it is that so often secular narrative artists give us fiction and it feels like the truth, while the Church gives us truth and it feels like fiction.

Recalling that it is *suspense* that maintains the story—and the sermon—it is not difficult to surmise the enormous power of credibility. People do not hold their breath over the insignificant, *nor* do they hold it if they think it will not be given back.

Ambiguity is the key and in its primary meaning has to do with the *not-yet-disclosed*. To be caught by it is to be torn among equally plausible views. One cannot be sure—yet. It is the suspension of revelation and decision. How will it turn out? Who perpetrated the crime? How will the hero survive the crisis? How can the gospel make a difference? This is ambiguity—known externally as conflict and internally as tension. As such, it is altogether different from the *ambiguous* in the sense of the *imprecise*.

Everyone knows the pain of listening to a preacher who after announcing the text or opening an issue does an inchoate slow (very slow) dance all over the room of the theme—all the while floating about two inches above the surface of the floor. Pretty soon all are convinced that either the preacher has forgotten the text or issue altogether or is making the supreme effort not to step directly on anything. Everything is related to everything else—sort of—and in the most general way. As a listener you cannot consent to the narrative trip because it is not clear—neither route nor destination, not even place of beginning. This is not an example of ambiguity, but of imprecision born of being ambiguous. The suspense of *not yet* gives way to the growing resignation of *not ever*!

Of course all of this points to the need for distinct clues provided throughout the sermonic process—being precise about the route, yet not announcing how in fact it will turn out. But here the primary point is different. I am talking about the trust factor as central to ambiguity. One of the finest storytellers I have ever had the pleasure to hear is my colleague Dr. Tex Sample, Professor of Church and Society at Saint Paul School of Theology—and a truly fine preacher. Often a sermon of his consists of three stories back to back. Once done the congregation has experienced the gospel. But, strangely, he does not make any transition between the stories. He just closes one down and opens the next. And everyone moves where he takes them. The reason is that somehow everyone knows that *he* knows exactly where he is going *and will arrive there*—and when the time is ripe so shall we. After the point is made everyone breathes again. In one sense I could "fault" him for lack of transitions (my homiletical views insist on doing so). But there is no reason for complaint.

Trust is the key. Its power rivets the attention of the congregation, and the story's own ambiguity does the rest.

A sermon's necessary ambiguity rests upon the consent of the congregation—a consent born of (1) the presence of something at stake, (2) the congregation's trust in the preacher to resolve the issue in light of the gospel, and (3) the preacher's withholding resolution until the proper time.

Now back to the question of the preacher being limited to what the congregation thinks important (at any given time). There are two quite important reasons why we need not assume the "obvious" conclusion about limited possible themes and necessarily optimistic views of human nature. The first reason again has to do with trust. When a congregation has grown accustomed to their pastor dealing with difficult issues, hidden issues, surprising issues, and truly leading them to wrestle with the gospel and human existence as they are led to recognize them, the resulting trust of past experiences now makes possible their giving the necessary consent to be led down the road of the narrative. One cannot expect that every Sunday the people come to worship carrying with them in unison the issue that the sermon addresses at that time. Often the preacher will take an unknown text and raise an unthought issue. With trust, people grant the consent, at least preliminarily (after all, our consent is not given just once in a sermon, but repeatedly). It is then up to the preacher to enlist the congregation's continual and growing consent to an ever escalating ambiguity.

The other reason that preaching as we are considering it does not become fenced in by the congregational expectations, views, and vested interests can be identified in the preaching style of Jesus. Barth notes the Bible's *nein* to our questions, but Jesus chose a different way to break the bad news. When asked a question—often right out of the vested interest of the questioner, he did not say: "Perhaps you should ask that another way" or "Here's the question you should have asked." He simply proceeded to tell a story—one that may or may not have appeared related to the question. The questioner could not get defensive—yet, could not argue. One had to wait and see—and then it was too late! For example: the man, after being told to love his neighbor, and live, asked: Well, please tell me, sir, who *is* my neighbor? That is, who has a claim on my life? Who must I help? Jesus answers: "There was a man who fell among thieves . . . " (Luke 10:29 paraphrase), and winds up telling the questioner *not* whom he should help—as though he had it together—but *who indeed* might have the capacity to help *him*! Why, he had no idea *he* was the one in the ditch! By means of the story Jesus really said: "Nein, wrong question!" But he didn't—and he did! A parable, or for that matter any story, has the capacity through a shift in location of time and place to address one question while talking about something else.

So, Fred Craddock, utilizing Kierkegaard's concept of indirect communication, speaks of "overhearing the gospel." The parables are superb examples of this technique of "blindsiding" our arrogance and our need. Craddock explains that another type of overhearing is the case of adults in congregations receiving more from children's sermons than the ones addressed to them—they think it is for someone else. Telling a story of oppression in some other place or time likewise can be powerful in addressing our own acts of oppression here and now. Nathan's conversation with David is the classic example of this kind of indirect communication. Of course we arm ourselves against the judgment of the gospel, and we are quick to rationalize our present life-style. The sense of our own righteousness is deepened by the quickness of our mind. We *are* clever; we define and explain away with remarkable skill! Then, the hammer of the gospel—when handled through parable or other story form—comes at the *end*, not the beginning of the sermon.

The Plot Thickens

Whenever we use the phrase "now the plot thickens" we acknowledge an accurate intuitive grasp of how narrative time works. The fact that a moving plot line seems to make things worse (with disequilibrium becoming increasingly removed from resolution) is something about which we all know. We've grown so accustomed to it via novels, detective stories, television, drama, and film that we take it for granted— except perhaps when we preach.

It takes only a small amount of disequilibrium to catch people's initial interest: "Once upon a time . . . " or "The other day when . . . " is all it takes. But this initial disequilibrium must then quickly be "swollen" (or "deepened" if you prefer). Things become more complicated. The potential solution that seemed just around the corner has now gained great distance; it may have become out of sight altogether.

The swelling of suspense—an outgrowth of the swelling of ambiguity—is not a difficult-to-grasp matter, either in identifying it or in accomplishing it. Recall if you will the last informal group conversation that started with the statement: "The trouble with the younger generation is . . ." or "The whole problem of poverty is simply that . . . " Do you remember how at first the answers came in droves— simple, clear, quick? Then someone added this variable, and another added that factor, and all of a sudden the certainty of solution became most elusive. The quick "pat" answer can be seriously entertained only as long as the issue is kept superficial—that is, simple. Every new variable adds both complication and depth. The more complicated, the deeper engaged, the more remote any answer seems to be, and hence the greater the ambiguity and suspense become. It's as simple as that.

Hence a novelist will give us a character or two and provide only enough data for us to make snap judgments. Then more incidents and character revelations are provided, and these do not confirm the earlier judgments. Pretty soon, we do not know what to think. She appeared so bad, immoral in behavior and attitude. So why now does she do the good deed, befriend the one everybody else is ignoring, etc.? The king plans a banquet, sends his servants to invite the good worthy guests, R.S.V.P. "Too busy," replies one: "previous commitment, sorry," another regrets. So "lesser" guests receive the only slightly used invitations. Finally the unthinkable ones arrive at the king's table. The person to whom the story is told thought the good and the bad quite easily discernible—*before* the story complicated things.

Likewise, Christians are called by the sermon to "love their neighbors." That's easy enough—until the small-town preacher looks out and spots there on the third row the Chevrolet dealer who is wondering what the admonition might mean in his relation to the Ford dealer, who just happens to be worshiping with another congregation down the street. (The preacher there is retelling the story of Jesus and the Samaritan woman at the well.) Things do get complicated, and suspense builds.

The first consequence of such complication for our preaching work is simply that the process of escalation needs to be shared *with* the congregation (rather than solved in the study and announced in the pulpit). But we who dare to proclaim the gospel have more yet going for us than the simple addition of variables. Two theological matters are particularly important. First, things are never what they seem. This conviction is at the very heart of the gospel. How else can it be that the Good News is folly to the Greeks and a stumbling block to the Jews? We all surely have noticed that Jesus seldom complimented the "good"—and seldom damned the "bad." And hardly was he cooperative in fulfilling the law's demand when presented with the woman taken in adultery. The conviction that things are not what they seem is not the simple result of tricky reality; it rests upon a deep flaw in human perception—a flaw we all share, particularly when quickly solving others' misbehavior. "Choose this day whom you will serve" (Josh. 24:15). But how many of our parishioners actually and consciously will to serve evil?

Moreover, the gospel has a way of replacing our cultural values and assumptions, often with the reverse. This is particularly true when the issue is the *will*. Even when not stated overtly, the underlying current of conviction in our culture is that anyone can do anything if the determination is there. "Where there's a will there's a way." It's All-American. "The difficult we do right away; the impossible takes a little longer." Recalling that group conversation when quick answers came like an avalanche, recall too that the first several pat answers most likely focused upon willpower.

Many of us who claim not to believe this tenet of faith act as though we do—particularly at stress points when our response is visceral. Even in our preaching, salvation by works is dominant—although camouflaged beautifully by most of us. We would not preach the heresy of work's righteousness bald-faced, of course. We do announce what God has done in Christ. Yet it is often *not* the dominant theme, and it tends to be cut off from the rest of the sermon—announced and then left stranded. Or we may connect the gospel in the following way: "Since we know that to find our lives is to lose them, and to lose our lives for the sake of the Gospel is to find them, let us therefore be about the task of losing them for Christ's sake. Then we shall . . ." (paraphrase of Mark 8:35). In short, our calculation about grace subverts its surprise, and grace is reduced to final reward for good efforts.

But we are not the first to be shocked by the radicality of grace. Norman Perrin notes the remarkable difference between the parables of Jesus and the Jewish proverbial sayings—which "shrink back" from the radicality of Jesus.[1] Also, the editorial comments, which often are placed in Jesus' mouth in the Synoptic accounts, typically serve to pull back to a more conventional morality. So we have an additional verse tacked onto the parable of the Good Samaritan, which admonishes us to "go and do likewise." This comment might have fit with the conversation Jesus and the lawyer were having before the story but makes little sense after the story is told.

Note, then, the factors that assist us in escalating the ambiguity with which the sermon has begun. First to ask questions, to increase the variables is both to increase the complexity of the issue and to heighten the suspense.

Moreover it heightens the credibility of the preacher, too, because down deep people know their lives are complicated. When after a sermon someone says to you: "I felt like somehow you knew all about me," what they probably mean is that you were true to their life's complexities. Second, the gospel's message that things are seldom what they seem serves to heighten the search for the way things really are in God's view. To believe this is to not settle for obvious culture-approved conclusions, but to probe further for the surprising revelatory view. Third, when the radicality of the gospel sweeps in, tables are turned, viewpoints are reversed, and suddenly the preacher and the congregation are experiencing the reversal of narrative that puts life together again. It seems so obvious *now*, but somehow could not have been anticipated in advance.

Dr. Roger Carstensen of the Christian church and a longtime leader in preaching workshops often has pastors take familiar sayings, biblical and otherwise, and asks them to "turn the coin over"—that is, to rephrase the saying in a sharply different, even reversed, way. The exercise is exceedingly valuable in helping us to see things in new, bold relief. Moreover the shock of surprise of the pastors is not just "understood" but felt, *experienced*. And it seems never to be the result of their calculations. To be sure, they intended to say the familiar with a new twist—even to literally turn it upside down, but the new twist comes as discovery not creation. So says Jesus: The last shall be first, and the first last (or the good last and the bad first)—and the hearers *had* to be shocked. And the point of the Workers in the Vineyard parable is not at all that some got paid correctly and others received a gift besides. It is that *none were paid*. All—the early and the late—received the gift of being invited home to the vineyard. What a shock to Peter, who with considerable spiritual arrogance had prompted the telling by having just asked: "What do we get?" (Matt. 19:27, paraphrase). The answer: "If one is in a calculating mood—*cheated!*"

Once the reversal of the gospel is experienced, new life can be anticipated. By means of reversal, a new profound simplicity overtakes the confusion that had succeeded the original pat simplicity. Said Oliver Wendell Holmes in explanation: "I do not give a fig for the simplicity this side of complexity, but I would give my life for the simplicity on the other side of complexity." The term "denouement" in narrative art—meaning "unraveling" (of suspense)—signals the time for resetting the table. The future now can be anticipated, and note that the new life, which is now possible, is provided by the action of God. The denouement phase is inaugurated by the *indicative* of the gospel, not the *imperative* of our commitment. Yet the indicative does indeed open the door so that now we *can* respond in commitment; not that by commitment we open the door ourselves.

The entire sweep of moving suspense as possible in a sermon merits a fuller discussion than we have just experienced. But since that sweep occupies the central thrust of my earlier volume, *The Homiletical Plot: The Sermon as Narrative Art Form*, I think it best not to repeat myself here. In that writing I attempt to take the reader through the entirety of the sermonic plot—step by step (actually five steps). Here the focus is on *time* and its impact upon a sermon shaped by its movement. We are just now ready for what I believe to be the most crucial issue of this chapter's concern regarding narrative time.

In particular I want to address what I presume surely must be a growing question by whatever typical preacher has happened onto these pages. The question begins with an affirmation (of sorts): "But, I am not a storyteller." "I am not a writer of fiction." "What does all this mean for me?" Or again, simply:

"What Story?"

The reason I presume the question is that constantly I have referred to the fictional narrative world, and I have drawn upon the parables of Jesus—which indeed are fictional too. Does all this mean that I am presuming that the typical preacher is going to dream up new parables Sunday after Sunday? Am I concluding that fictional story is the one and only legitimate form of the sermon? Or, am I suggesting that we limit our preaching to the parables of Jesus?

The answer is *no* to all three questions. Personally I would be panicked to have to invent a fictional story every Sunday—perhaps any Sunday! I do recommend the parables of Jesus for our sermon work, but hardly expect that all, or even most, of our sermons would be based on them. Moreover this is not a book about literature as such—either from our pen or anyone else's. My purpose in drawing from the field of narrative art is simply to borrow their powerful principles and techniques for our purpose in proclaiming the Word. It is narrative *form* that should interest us, not fiction as such. And it is narrative artists' utilization of that immediate data of experience called time that prompts my writing. My conclusion is that anytime we step behind a pulpit we are narrative artists. And what we call a sermon is best labeled *Story*, The Story, heard in the congregation.

The potentially powerful consequence of this can best be assessed by returning to the opening scene of the imaginary play with which I began this chapter. Remember, it is 8:10 P.M. and we are at the theater. Let us pick up our discussion at the point when I spoke of the playwright's task of drawing story time from one side—that fictional world (Chicago) that covered eighteen months—and from the other side enlisting the various times of the audience, which even included "past events" (Cleveland 1973, Madison 1980).

Now to be sure this imaginary playwright was creating a fictional world. But suppose we step into the playwright's place and fashion a narrative that instead of being fictional *is actually a portion of the real world of our parishioners*. Just like the playwright we will reach on the one side for story time, and likewise we will pick up the various inner times of the parishioners. But both are drawn from the *same side*.

Again, the story time may encompass eighteen months or perhaps the last eighteen years; it will be as selective as was the playwright's story time, perhaps more so because we will want to utilize one particular thread of the real world of our parishioners. Story time for our sermon will be compressed like the playwright's story time, only into twenty minutes of narrative time instead of two and a half hours of narrative time.

Now the point of all this is that while eliminating the fictional ingredient, we have yet maintained the form of story. And the principles of opening disequilibrium, escalating ambiguity, and the surprising (reversing) turn, and denouement carry the narrative to its conclusion. Narrative time next Sunday may be based on a lectionary passage or on a contemporary issue—but rather than the text being handled in the typical expository manner it will follow the changing stages of the plot; or again, instead of the topical sermon being outlined with introduction, three points, and a conclusion, it too will follow the stages of the plot. We will not likely "break into character" as a play does, but we will narrate a story in the same sense as a novelist does—except this is for real. In fact, writers of historical novels are often doing something very close to what I am suggesting. Buechner's *Godric*, (his latest novel) for example, is a historical novel based on a saint of the twelfth century. Our "saints" will be closer to home, and (unlike historical novels) left unnamed.

We too can locate the *setting* by making the sermon relate to the actualities of the real world of time and place. By means of our analysis of human nature we will be involved in the development of *character* and *action*. Our theological convictions will automatically be at work in the *tone*, and the story will move by means of *plot*. Indeed we will be saying much of the same things we would otherwise say, except that the evocative power of narrative form will prompt new angles of vision and particularize our proclamation of the gospel. The principle of narrative form, *moving suspense*, will be determining how and in what order we say what we say. In short, we will be *ordering experience in time* instead of *ordering ideas in space*. Narrative time—the sermon time—will enlist the power of *time* in the preaching of the Word.

In so doing, we will not be *inventing* a new form of preaching but *returning* to the biblical form—where story is the key (and not just in the parables)—whether in the call of Abraham, the description by Isaiah of proper worship and improper living, the rebellion of Jonah, the call of the disciples, the Damascus road, or the walk to Golgotha. All these are set in the form we are presently discussing. Whenever we pick up the Scriptures *we* are picked up into story time.

Chapter Five

THE BIBLE AND TIME

We should not be surprised that when H. Richard Niebuhr was ready to define the meaning of revelation in his classic work he should entitle the chapter "The Story of Our Life."[1] "We may remind ourselves," he noted, that "despite many efforts to set forth Christian faith in metaphysical and ethical terms of great generality, the only creed that has been able to maintain itself in the church with any approach to universality consists for the most part of statements about events." In this regard the Bible is our normative model, not only in presenting the narrative of God's ways with us through epic story, prophetic utterance, and parable, but also in its more formal "God talk." "Even God was defined," observes Niebuhr, "less by . . . metaphysical and moral character than by . . . historical relations, as the God of Abraham, Isaac and Jacob." To be a biblical preacher is to continue that tradition and participate in the history of telling the Story. But in recent times, at least among mainline Protestant groups, this has not been the case.

Amos Wilder has been one of the voices in our time lamenting what he calls "a long addiction to the discursive, the rationalistic, and the prosaic."[2] Canon Browne carries the complaint further: "Many who deny the literal inspiration of the Scriptures govern their work as preachers by doctrinal principles which assume that divine revelation is given in propositions. The form of their sermons denies implicitly what they state explicitly about the mode of revelation."[3] And Dan

Otto Via, whose work with the parables of Jesus are among the most important of our time, notes that "a Christian metaphysic would include the Bible as a basic model, image, or configuration which is to a large extent nonpropositional."[4] But to respond to these writers seriously the typical preacher must of necessity ask some questions we are not accustomed to asking. For if we have been too prosaic, and if in the Bible divine revelation is not couched primarily in propositions, what do we mean by the gospel's truth? It seems that all of a sudden the bottom has dropped out from under all we do in the pulpit.

If we do not speak propositionally, what on earth do we have to say? "God is love"—is that not propositional? "God was in Christ reconciling the world unto himself"—is that not propositional? In fact I can imagine the poor reader now—first being told to do *time* in the pulpit not *space*, then admonished to preach *narratively* not *topically*, and now summoned to be true to the biblical revelation, which is largely *nonpropositional*! One might suppose the next image will be that of preacher as poet (which is exactly what both Buechner and Browne propose)! But we are ahead of ourselves.

Actually the matter is not as confusing as it might appear, and the issue of what is meant by *nonpropositional* is first on our agenda. Later, after we have examined the issue and defined some terms, we will turn to biblical metaphor and parable to see how they embody what we are talking about.

I believe the term *nonpropositional* does not mean *anti-propositional*. To claim the biblical record to be largely nonpropositional is not to claim there are no biblical propositions. It is to say, first of all, that the Christian revelation as experienced historically in the corporate body of Christ, the church, simply cannot be contained in propositional form. *At best*, propositional statements viewed formally can be no more than dead skeletons of what once was lived experience. The *life* of the Good News runs so deep and spreads so broad that the linguistic form of conceptual thought only points in the direction of truth. The *more* of which we are all witnesses becomes *so much more* that at long last it is truer to speak of the difference in qualitative rather than quantitative terms.

At worst, propositional thought by its very nature distorts and even reforms the experiential meaning so that it is scarcely recognizable. Niebuhr says it is one thing to perceive "from a safe distance the occurrence in a stranger's life, and quite a different thing to ponder the path of one's own destiny." He illustrates by imagining the case history of a blind man healed, as recorded on the one hand by the attending surgeon, contrasted with the autobiographic account on the other hand, which barely mentions the surgical procedures utilized but tells "what happened to a self that had lived in darkness and now saw again . . . children's faces and the eyes of a friend."

Now if you can imagine the near impossibility of the former blind person sharing in propositional thought the meaning of that personal experience, you are in touch with what is meant in affirming that the Bible is largely nonpropositional. (You are also—potentially—in touch with what powerful preaching is all about.) And if you have had such an experience as Niebuhr relates (or anything close to it) you will recall when and where meaning occurred. Perhaps you went to church and were overwhelmed in the singing of "Amazing Grace"—and not at all because of the particularities of the propositional content of the third stanza. Or you scribbled a poem one day to express your meaning, perhaps using metaphorical language. Or you went to a movie and discovered a story that *was* your story. Such experiences are not void of cognition, they are not reducible to emotion (although emotion arises from them), and they are not anti-propositional. They represent a form of knowing that is *non*propositional. I call it aesthetic knowing and aesthetic language as contrasted with discursive knowing and discursive language.

With this definition I must emphasize an important denial—long made by poets, musicians, and other artists. "There is a current and exceedingly stupid doctrine," said

Austin Farrer in *A Rebirth of Images*, "that symbol evokes emotion and exact prose states reality. Nothing could be further from the truth: exact prose abstracts from reality, symbol presents it."[5] Says Wilder: "Before the message must be the vision, before the sermon the hymn, before the prose the poem."[6] "For the poem is not a statement but a performance of forces," say Ciardi and Williams, and "not an essay on life but a reenactment."[7] Buechner brings this same point to the task of the pulpit and to that potential miracle the congregation is waiting for, namely that the preacher "will not just *say* that God is present, because they have heard it said before and it has made no great and lasting difference to them," but rather that the preacher "will somehow make it real to them."[8]

To Make It Real

The difference between discursive and aesthetic knowing and the difference between proposition and presentation can be discerned by recalling the differing cognitive functions that occur, for example, in reading a book and experiencing a painting. With the book one is actively pursuing meaning. You attempt to understand; *grasp* the propositional thought. You desire to "get it." The painting also conveys cognitive meaning, but of a different kind. And if anything is "grasped," it is you! You do not attempt to understand by means of active volition. Rather you stay in its presence, and the "activity" is experienced as occurring at the other end. The painting takes *you* into *it*!

Eliseo Vivas, the aesthetic epistemologist, describes this latter experience as "intransitive attention," which sometimes results in a "complete revelation."[9] (Strange language coming from a secular art theorist!) Recently, Robert Ornstein has gained considerable recognition for his thesis regarding right and left lobe brain functions, maintaining that the left lobe is involved in typical, rational (propositional) functions while the right lobe centers in aesthetic, intuitive functions. If his thesis holds, one might say that what is being said about the Bible as nonpropositional is to say the biblical revelation demands right lobe functioning. But regardless of the outcome of the discussion on his claims, I find it most curious that many years before, when Jerome Bruner wrote about the intuitive, gestaltive form of cognition in the book *On Knowing*, strangely, he subtitled his work *Essays for the Left Hand*.[10]

But our concern here is not to second-guess the place in our brain where such functions occur; it is to identify the differences between discursive and aesthetic knowing. The former follows the grammar of our Greco-Roman type language system, ordering thought serially and resulting in what we call propositional thought. The latter form of knowing is gestaltive, taking place in revelatory events, and results in intuitive flashes of thought. Susanne Langer speaks of discursive and presentational forms.[11] Underneath both forms of knowing, I believe, are preconscious images that screen our receipt of "information." (Kenneth Boulding speaks of them in the book *The Image*,[12] but does not emphasize the preconscious nature of them.) We live by our preconscious images of reality (Susanne Langer speaks of them as fantasies) until one of them gets shoved aside in what seems an abrupt change. When that happens the only adequate term for it is *conversion*. (Strangely, when Boulding sought a good illustration of the replacement of one image by another, he chose religious conversion). Gordon Allport, in *Becoming*, spoke of the "sudden shift of propriate striving" when what was learned perhaps mechanically, and which seemed "cold, 'out there,' 'not mine,' " suddenly becomes "hot and vital, 'in here,' and 'mine.' "[13] He too utilized religious conversion as an example. The peculiar power of art is that its resultant aesthetic form communicates with us all at the preconscious level of our images. Otherwise put, a painting arises out of a painter's preconscious knowing and is received by an observer's preconscious knowing. The result is a deeply powerful understanding, not well explainable in ordinary language. Said one art form observer to the artist: "I don't know what you *said*, but I know what you mean." That is why one can speak of having been grasped by a work of art. That is also why if we are to consider the Bible as largely non-propositional and our preaching as aesthetic communication, we would do well to examine art forms and their nonpropositional means of meaning. Perhaps as a result we shall discover why Jesus spoke by means of parable.

Understanding the nature of poetry can be particularly helpful to us preachers, because while the poet uses "discursive" words, the poet does so in a non-discursive way.

Eliseo Vivas says the poet is a midwife who brings into being that which was only latently real before. "A poet's words," says Wallace Stevens, "are of things that do not exist without the words." Buechner insists that truth itself "cannot finally be understood but only experienced. It is the experience that they stun us with speaking it out in poetry which transcends all other language in its power to open the doors of the heart." In fact, "they do not say something as much as they make something happen."[14]

The crucial distinction between linguistic and aesthetic communication is summarized by Ciardi and Williams when they explain that "no matter how serious the overt message of a poem, the unparaphraseable and undiminishable life of the poem lies in the way it performs itself . . . The *way* in which it means *is* what it means" (italics mine). So it is, as Via suggests, that "language can become an event." Indeed, Sallie McFague TeSelle sees this possibility to be the central feature of a parable, that "it is itself what it is talking about."[15]

All of which is to say to us who preach, that anytime we launch into story, even if simply for purpose of illustration, we launch ourselves and our congregations into the aesthetic mode of communication—a mode which is both deeply precise and yet never quite explainable in propositional terms. Put simply, I am asserting that when preaching turns narrative it always says more than we know (propositionally) and hence potentially opens the door for deep calling unto deep.

Moreover, this fact has negative as well as positive possibilities—indeed it can be discerned most readily when it happens counterproductively. Recall the time you chose to "spice up" a sermon point by the use of an illustration—one that seemed just right to concretize the point you would be making? Except that when it happened that Sunday morning you sensed that you and the congregation entered the story together, but you moved on alone. They seemed to stay with the story, lingering, while you were advancing to the next point. It is quite possible that the problem was not that the story was confusing or not on target. It might have been that the story was larger than the point being made by it. It occasioned an event, and the congregation's intransitive attention to its "poetic" message precluded their moving on with your prose.

The closing lines of Robert Frost's "Stopping by Woods on a Snowy Evening" will help our understanding here:

> The woods are lovely, dark, and deep
> But I have promises to keep
> And miles to go before I sleep
> And miles to go before I sleep.

The first three lines serve to summarize the entire poem, and can be taken pretty much at face value. But when the third line is repeated, everything changes. *More* is meant here than first met the eye or ear, and its power is not simply that the referent is widened beyond the day's experiences. We now know, perhaps suddenly, that the whole poem is larger and deeper than we first knew, and the reader or listener must now reprocess the whole poem. Paul Ricoeur would explain that we have been confronted "with a language which says more than what it says, which says something other than what it says and which, consequently, grasps [us] because it has in its meaning created a new meaning."[16] Imagine what would happen if Frost made the mistake of adding another verse to the poem. He would travel alone, for we are too occupied with the event of the last line.

I trust the reader will not presume a false conclusion here. I am not suggesting that we ought to avoid illustrative material because when we do we are playing with power. Quite the reverse! I am asserting that the aesthetic power of story impels us to think of the entire sermon as story. When the sermon by its very form is narrative, this power turns words into events, preachers into poets, and God language into religious experience. Narrative preaching can *make it real*. And the Bible, through metaphor and parable, shows us how.

Parable: An Extended Metaphor

"With many such parables he spoke the word to them," said Mark the evangelist; in fact "he did not speak to them without a parable" (4:33, 34). Crossan concludes: "Jesus' parables are radically constitutive of his own distinctive historicity and all else is located in them." TeSelle even speaks of "Jesus as the parable of God." Obviously, then, the preacher who intends to be a biblical preacher needs to grasp the meaning and power of parabolic preaching. But the peculiar form of narrative preaching utilized by Jesus in the parables is not given to simple definition.

Back in seminary days I thought I knew exactly what the term meant—identifiable by contrasting it with allegory. Allegories, I was told, are stories that appear to talk about ordinary experiences, except there is an extraordinary set of connections to something else, which is the real subject under discussion. Sometimes that connection is a secret—hidden until disclosed by someone who has the key. Then of course everything is understandable. *This* represents *that* and *these* represent *those*. I have sometimes been summoned by my doorbell and greeted at the front door by someone—Bible in hand—who is happy to tell me the secret connection of an alleged allegorical passage in the book of Revelation that the person claims really refers to a current event! The parable, on the other hand, doesn't make those intricate this-means-that connections; it makes a single point, I once learned. Hence, as soon as the parable of the sower is explained to me—that the rocky ground stands for the ones whose hearing of the Word finds worldly pleasures and wealth overpowering competitors—then I know the one-point parable has been turned into an allegory. But either way, parable or allegory, there was a definitive propositional truth to be secured.

But now TeSelle says that thinking of a parable as an extended metaphor means "not that the parable 'has a point' or teaches a lesson, but that it is itself what it is talking about." Via speaks of parables "in the broad general sense" and then identifies the three major classes: similitude, example story, and parable (in the limited sense). A similitude such as the Lost Coin tells of a woman who lost one of her coins and set about to find it, which by comparison illustrates the proper ways of God and us. The Pharisee and the Publican is an example story and doesn't need comparison—the point is included in the story and we are called to respond accordingly. A parable in the narrow sense of the term, says Via, is "a freely invented story" that is "not concerned with what everyone typically does but narrates a particular thing," which stands by itself as a "real aesthetic object." More precisely, Via explains "there is more than one important element in a parable, and all of these features must be given consideration, but they do not relate primarily and in the first place to an event, events, or ideas outside of the parable. They relate first of all to each other within the parable." Whatever matters the parable is concerned with—and there may be more than one—are communicated *indirectly*, as TeSelle explains. "The story is 'thick,' not transparent; like a painting, it is looked *at* not through." Because "meaning is held in solution in the metaphor" the truth is *inside not outside*.

But the radical difference between these contemporary writers and the concept of parable as one point, with which I was raised, has to do *not* just with the location of the referent but also with its epistemological mode—its form of meaning. Whatever one's definition, obviously a parable includes a referent *beyond* the experiences related in the story. And the crucial distinction above has to do with whether the *sense* of that beyond is simply referred to (pointed) or whether it is intrinsic to the story. Perrin describes this difference as between "through-meaning" and "in-meaning."[17]

But note also that "in–meaning" is not propositionally articulatable in the same sense as "through-meaning." That *beyond-that-is-inside* seems to have no limits of depth. You cannot capture its essence and place propositional fences around it. When Frost said "and miles to go before I sleep" the in-meaning has an almost infinite depth of possibility (Ricoeur would say "inexhaustible"). Yet it does not become obscure or indefinite. The well simply will not run dry. Two quite different readers at the surface level attach quite different experiences, contexts, and expectations to Frost's lines. Yet at a deeper level they share a common reality. And when the pop country singer reminds us that we were not promised a rose garden, we all *know*—differently, and yet the same.

The peculiar power of a simple metaphor—defined as "the verbal recognition of a similarity between the apparently dissimilar,"[18] becomes even more profoundly powerful when extended into the form of a parable. This is so because a simple metaphor typically utilizes objects-in-space (rose gardens) whereas the parable by means of story also utilizes events-in-time (the journey of the prodigal son). But how is it that the meaning can be infinite in depth and yet not indefinite in content?

The Image

If it is true, as I suggested earlier, that underneath both linguistic and aesthetic modes of knowing resides a set of largely preconscious images of reality that screen the input of data, and if it is true that an aesthetic form communicates primarily from the artist's images to the beholder's images, then the connection of parable told and received is primarily preconscious in nature. Put simply, we hear with our images of reality, just as the artists communicate with theirs. Little wonder, then, that artists of all forms witness to their handling of meanings that outrun their intentions and purposes (and why a poet can be called a midwife). Likewise, the beholder of a particular work of art is often frustrated when the chance comes to interview the artist to check out the accuracy of the beholder's interpretation of meaning: "Is this what you intended to say?" comes the query—often greeted by a blank stare or perhaps a question in return: "Is this what it means to you?" People often take this last kind of comment to mean that there really is no objective meaning or intent—that a work of art means whatever one chooses for it to mean. Not so. What this kind of interchange really contains is the artist's refusal to state what cannot be articulated proposition-ally. Sometimes artists are both surprised and impressed with the profundity of their discovery *after* it has been made and presented to the world. Said playwright Neil Simon: "Writing is like walking through a forest and not knowing what you're going to meet next." One day after writing about the character Stanley, Simon announced to his wife that he had had a fantastic day "because Stanley worked it all out." H. Grady Davis is suggesting the same phenomenon when he says that a sermon has a life of its own.[19]

Yet it surely becomes obvious that this discussion raises a number of questions, the most important one being: How can this be? If things happen beyond the control of the artist, who cannot even tell you precisely what is meant; if a parable can be infinite in depth while not indefinite in content, and if two people of quite different personal histories when exposed to the same work of art can receive meaning particular to each yet common to both, then what strange, perhaps mystical variable is involved?

Henry Mitchell calls it the *transconscious*. Borrowing the term from Mircea Eliade and drawing some features from Jung, Mitchell identifies how it is that the black preacher is able to tap common roots that empower the sermon: "The art of black preaching is not *less* than logical; it is logical on more *levels* or wave lengths, addressing . . . the obvious mentality and the subtle mentality called the unconscious by some, but more accurately the intuition."[20] Hence, when the black preacher opens the Bible, finds the text, and says, "I have been a stranger in a strange land" (Exod. 2:22), the observation of Moses turned metaphor connects not only with the particulars of personal experience but with the commonality of oppression everywhere, and everyone in the congregation *knows*.

What Mitchell calls the transconscious I call the preconscious image—that form of knowing that occurs just underneath the limits of propositional thought and often evoked by aesthetic objects and events. The black preacher can evoke the meaning intentionally, both because of highly developed expertise and because of the particulars of minority experience. But preconscious images are not the sole possession of any one group. All of us have them at our disposal—even if we have not cultivated their use.

The poet knows how—and so did Jesus. When he said that "the younger son gathered all he had and took his journey into a far country" (Luke 15:13), we understand. Well, a lot of us do. For those who have never taken the trip, Jesus added a brother who "was angry and refused to go in" (Luke 15:28). And one does not have to be born on a farm in order to be grasped powerfully by the metaphorical language of the psalmist: "The Lord is my shepherd, I shall not want" (Psalm 23:1).

Just because our images are hidden from view doesn't mean they do not operate powerfully. In fact they may be the more powerful because we are unable to control them at the conscious level. Have you ever happened to notice, for example, that when you are in a crowded room and spot a person some distance away whom you have met previously but cannot now identify by name, that although you cannot recall where or when or under what circumstances the personal encounter occurred, you nonetheless know quite certainly whether this is friend or foe. You have internalized an image that remains long after conscious recognition slips away.

I am convinced that these many images—some drawn from the relatively common experiences of one's own group and others drawn from the universals of human experience—are the basic raw material that makes aesthetic experiences so powerful. Whether the artist has chosen the words or colors on purpose, or whether the words or colors seem to have chosen the artist, the result is that powerful experience that sometimes surprises not only the beholder but even the artist.

If this is true, as I believe, then one can understand what H. Grady Davis means in saying a sermon has a life of its own. It means that once sermon preparation has begun the story can unfold according to the dictates of those universals we know at the preconscious level. Of course Stanley worked it out for Neil Simon, because Simon was wise enough at the conscious level to stand aside and let it happen. "Stay in the presence of the characters," [21]Beuchner advises, and they—informed by your images of human nature and experience—will finally let you in on the conclusion.

The power of biblical metaphor and parable is due in considerable measure to the optimal form they provide for allowing imagic connections to be made. And the result of hearing a parable of Jesus is not having fictional characters of first-century Palestine come alive, but rather to rediscover oneself!

But the power of metaphor is not limited to parabolic form in the narrow sense. Anytime you tell a story, you open the door for metaphor to operate. When, for example, you describe the apprehension a child experiences in moving to a new school, you have done more than describe moving to a new school. You have produced a metaphor that touches images of apprehension throughout the congregation. You may not have intended to address that person who is about to retire from the railroad (or again you may have so intended) and that person may not be able to identify just what the connection was. Perhaps the response at the door after the service is simply an unusually warm handshake and the words "thank you," but the impact—however undefined propositionally—happened. The sermon event occurred.

Moreover, if we perceive all preaching as story—an ordering of experience—and shape our sermons in narrative form, we maximize the possibilities for aesthetic communication, for metaphor to happen. The good poet, say Ciardi and Williams, "enact[s] his experience rather than . . . talk[ing]about having had them. '*Show* it, don't *tell* it,' he says, 'make it happen, don't talk about its happening.' " The same is true for the good preacher. Parables show it; metaphors make it happen.

Of course, Neil Simon *could* stand aside and let it happen; after all he is a great writer. So could Robert Frost. What about us common preachers who likely will never make a claim to fame—and who must do our work on schedule, week after week? How do you learn how to allow it to happen? The question, if it is real, is actually a question about how one goes about preparing the sermon. It is a question about the *creative process* itself. And to this theme we now turn.

Chapter Six

PREPARATION, CREATIVITY, AND TIME

Talking to narrative artists (including preachers) about *how* they do what they do often is more frustrating than illuminating. Generally they will concede they do not know how it is that they are creative and sometimes express surprise that others cannot be the same. Just "stay in the presence of the characters"[1] advises Buechner regarding the writing of novels; but this answer may provide more questions than answers.

Clearly, a common thread I have heard in comments from creative people is the notion of *listening* or *being led*—drawn forward by some unnamed reality not of their own making. This elusive quality has resulted in the conclusion regarding creativity, that "some have it and some don't," and that is the end of the matter. Skill is teachable, the logic goes, but art is a gift.

I happen both to believe and yet not believe this conclusion. Certainly some people have intuitively fallen into patterns of artistic preparation that result in creativity. Not knowing precisely what the variables are, these creative people often are unable to identify them for the sake of others. Yet, I believe some of those variables are in fact identifiable. Moreover, I believe creativity is not something one *has*, but rather something one *allows*—that is, creativity is not a unique active resource one calls on directly by intention, but rather, a passive capacity—shared in considerable degree *both* by those labeled "creative" and those not so labeled. In short I am suggesting that creativity is not a *thing* given to a few, but a *possible result* for the many.

Finley Eversole, in *The Politics of Creativity*, provides the remarkable conclusion that "in our society, at the age of five, 90 percent of the population measures 'high creativity.' By the age of seven, the figure has dropped to 10 percent. And the percentage of adults with high creativity is only two percent."[2] These statistics suggest that we may be considering a capacity that most of us have *lost* rather than a capacity we never found or had. The credibility of this view is immediately confirmable by our own observation regarding storytelling.

Most of us were quite good at storytelling when we were young. Two small children get together to play, quickly decide the roles each will assume (e.g., cops and robbers), and the story flies. Or, one child alone with time but no playmate (nor TV!) will quickly decide on a setting and characters, and the plot emerges. An adult, asked to repeat the childhood art known so well years before, will freeze in terror.

Just why there is this strange difference between the creativity of childhood and the lack of creativity among adults—so well attested by our own experiences—is provided a clue by Madeleine L'Engle's observation that during creative activity "the artist lets go the self control he normally clings to and is open to riding the wind." Maslow observes similarily that creative people appear to be "less controlled and inhibited in their behavior than the average."[3]

The culprit behind the fact of adults being more inhibited than children, according to George B. Leonard, is our formal education process, which he says succeeds in "damming up the flood of human potentialities." He explains further:

> Schools and colleges have until now . . . served a society that needed reliable, predictable human components. Appropriately enough, they spent overwhelming amounts of time and energy ironing out those human impulses and capabilities that seemed errant. Since learning involves behavioral change, lifelong learning was the most errant of behaviors and was not

to be countenanced. Educational institutions, therefore, were geared to *stop* learning.[4]

Certainly, with the growth of specialized disciplines, the push of aesthetics to the periphery of the classroom, the reductionistic concept of art as emotion, there is little wonder that five-year-olds are more creative than adults, and that the natural capacity for creativity is dulled, even thwarted by the time we reach "maturity"! But before exploring further the phenomenon of "letting go"—its *what, how,* and *when*—we need to add other variables to the mix of our concern, drawing from those who have studied creativity, such as Maslow, May, and Rogers.

If talking to creative artists leaves one unenlightened about our present concern, turning to the experts leaves one confused. Carl Rogers, for example, is convinced that although creativity and neuroses may stem from the same source, "creativity tends to flow best in the absence of neuroses."[5] Maslow agrees, seeing a connection "between creativity . . . and the . . . integration of one's self."[6] But then, how do you account for Beethoven, Hooke, Van Gogh, Baudelair, Heine, Wagner, and others, asks Frank Barron, who is "unwilling to accept overall psychological health as the criterion for a creative person."[7] The creative giants of the world simply are not explainable as the most well adjusted!

My personal knowledge of a large number of preachers will not sustain the notion of a positive relationship between psychological health and creativity; if anything the reverse would be more likely! And artistic creativity among groups often emerges out of oppression—witness the emergence of jazz out of the despair of American slavery. By comparison the plantation owners had "relative absence of fear" and hence should have displayed creative "behavior . . . less blocked" (to use Maslow's norms)—but no great art form emerged from that group. The phrase "necessity is the mother of invention" surely suggests something deeper than psychological adjustment as the ground for creativity.

Certainly if all other factors were removed, then the "well adjusted" ought to be less inhibited than the "average." But, is it possible that "openness" towards one's own ideas is a helpful but secondary ingredient in the profile of creativity?

I believe Rollo May would answer in the affirmative, noting as he does that "creativity arises out of the tension between spontaneity and limitation" and recalling Alfred Adler's proposal "that civilization arose out of our physical limitations."[8] In order to identify the genesis of creativity May provides the helpful image of a river that requires both water and the containment of a riverbank. The "water" of spontaneity certainly would include such subjective factors as "openness" and "lack of inhibition," but more objective factors such as "requiredness" and "necessity"—the result of the impact of containment—are also included, and I believe they are more primary. Certainly, such a view assists in explaining how the art form of jazz would arise from among the slaves rather than the slave-owners. And May's river image of water and river bank can be pressed toward even greater explanatory utility relative to this crucial factor of interior and/or objective necessity as regarding creativity.

By avocation I am a jazz pianist, and I find that I am more creative at the keyboard when two factors are present: (1) pain and (2) grace. If, for example, I arrive home facing a difficult personal or professional issue, I am inevitably drawn to the piano. And I play the blues—regardless of what I play. The result is never therapy. Playing the piano does not remove any negative reality; but it does give objective form to interior forces. Depression is never lifted (though sometimes deepened); but it is always refined. At such moments I understand—if only by poor analogy—the ingredient of pain as related to creativity. The river banks of constraint squeeze the force of the stream into powerful expression. It is the in-spite-of yearning for resurrection over death, of freedom over oppression, the triumph of order over chaos (this last being a paraphrase of Leonard Bernstein's definition of music). Without the pathos of the valley as an internal touchstone, creativity is seldom more than cleverness. Without this touchstone, the preacher preaches in vain.

Grace is the other ingredient. Sometimes I am called to sit in with a group of musicians whose pianist is temporarily absent, and I always hope the other musicians in the group are not too good—not alone for my ego's sake, but for music's sake. Even when the other musicians mask their disdain for my best attempt as substitute, I still see judgment in their eyes, and my fingers turn to thumbs. Self-consciousness drains my capacity for creativity, and I barely survive the evening. I need either to be approved for my skill—or loved in spite of its lack. At home I am loved. Late in the evening I will sit down with only Sarah, my wife, to hear—and it's all right! She hears the music of my soul, not the limited skill of my hands. Sometimes I will close my eyes and listen to the surprises my hands create—literally striking notes I really had not intended, but which then suggest musical motifs I never could have willed. Kindly, Sarah will reveal her regret that we did not record those moments of musical surprise. But the recorder has no grace to offer, and hence the music never could have led me into its way. The phrase "playing over one's head" is inverted; it is playing under one's head.

All of which raises a crucial question: Have I not just described two conditions for creativity that are beyond our control and hence none too helpful in supporting my allegation that creativity is not simply a gift that is beyond our power to evoke or will? On the face of it, it would seem so. If one is more creative in the presence of (1) pain and (2) grace, then should we not with a sense of helplessness concede that some will have these ingredients present on occasion—and some will not? I believe such a conclusion to be false.

Recalling the artists' witness to "letting go" and "being led," and remembering the greater creativity we had as children, we can now consider the ingredients of pain and grace in a new way. Whatever the models for creativity, "the theme of unguarded unconscious," says Adams, "surfaces again and again."[9] The question, therefore, is not: Can one *will* to be creative? The question becomes: Can one *choose certain behaviors* that will have the result of removing the guards our consciousness has placed on the unconscious? And to this new question, I believe the answer is *yes*! But before we proceed further, I need to identify some unstated assumptions relative to our experience of pain and grace.

First, pain. My consciousness knows pain on an *off* and *on* basis. Today I am "up"; tomorrow perhaps "down." Today I may concentrate on a problem and feel the pain of frustration. Tomorrow the result is joy in fulfillment. But, I am convinced, my subconscious—or better, my preconscious—carries a vast reservoir of pain, drawn from past experiences. (Only my consciousness really forgets.) My preconscious understands that my tidy conscious summary of life is a mask that survival wears. The deep human spirit continues to cry in life's brokenness and ambiguity long after consciousness has found the happy solution either of denial or victory. When the poet speaks of being led, note the leading moves into gaps of ambiguity. It is the "not yet" of the preconscious world that informs the work, and creativity can emerge. And the preacher's theme of victory through Christ will stay superficial unless the preacher can be open to the disquieting voice of the preconscious, which at the very least can remember when it was not so! In this sense every preacher must become *lost* in the process of preparing the sermon that announces our being *found*. Little wonder we guard our preconscious. It knows too much!

And now to grace. The adage "better to be thought a fool than to open your mouth and have people know for certain" is an absolute antidote against creativity. Behind our guard, undergirded so well by educational processes and our cultural understanding of "maturity," lies that "better safe than sorry" assumption that results in utter control. Theologically put, we have been taught that we must be found worthy. But that is not what we preach—and better yet, it is not what we have learned in deep experiences of love. That is why I can play the piano with abandon in the presence of my wife; she loves me anyway! The preconscious remembers these experiences of grace too, and the resultant wholeness of self that ensues. And the preconscious has not been sworn to consistency. It holds all of it together—the pain *and* the grace, the suffering and the overcoming. It is all there—waiting not to be performed, but to be released. Hence the question now is: Can it be released, and if so, how and when and where?

Creativity and Sermon Preparation

I now intend, therefore, by focusing on sermon preparation time, to be quite specific in answering the question of how we can be more creative preachers. These suggestions are based on the three key convictions already discussed: first, that creativity is not something a few people have but rather a potential result we all possess to considerable degrees; second, that although one cannot will directly to be creative (any more than one can will to "be spontaneous now"), one *can* choose certain behaviors that will maximize our creative powers waiting to be unleashed; and third, that the key to creativity lies in releasing the creative preconscious mind from the controls of routine consciousness—a consciousness particularly inhibited among us clergy who are paid to have tidy answers to the world's untidy needs.

Rollo May identifies the first variable or factor when he tells his own story of particularly rich moments of creativity (and in the context of this time-centered writing we might note how important *time* is to his understanding of creativity). May notes that creativity is most likely to get loose *when* one has first spent considerable time in highly focused, intensive, and conscious deliberation of the issues at hand. "The unconscious breakthrough," May explains, "requires the alternation of intense, conscious work and relaxation," and, typically, creative insight "comes at a moment of transition between work and relaxation."[10] After hard deliberation in sermonic preparation, for example, it is then time to let go of the matter altogether. Do something else that requires a different kind of concentration on some utterly unrelated activity. May tells the story of his frustration of having a research study hypothesis fail miserably when tested. He could not solve his "insoluble problem." But, "late one day, putting aside my books and papers in the little office I used . . . I walked down the street toward the subway. I was tired. I tried to put the whole troublesome business out of my mind. About fifty feet away from the entrance to the Eighth Street station, it suddenly struck me 'out of the blue,' as the not-unfitting expression goes"—and he knew immediately what was wrong with his earlier hypothesis, and said "I think I had not taken another step on the sidewalk when a whole new hypothesis broke loose in my mind."[11]

In the context of sermon preparation, the lectionary-based preacher will need to read carefully the lections for the next Sunday in every available translation and paraphrase (and in original language texts if the preacher is so equipped). I believe it is important at this point of preparation *not* to consult the exegetical experts, as they will impose their uncreative mental ruts on the preacher, who at this point in preparation time is attempting to get loose, not be tied down! It is important then to select what appears the most problematic issue raised in or by the text and to wrestle with determination for considerable time—but allowing no final conclusion to be reached. Following May's experience and writing, the preacher should work, not until something is solved but until something clearly is most *un*solved.

It is at the point of considered quandary, of intensive irresoluteness, that the preacher should drop the matter altogether, leave the study, and become absorbed in some activity quite unrelated: a hospital call, some administrative task, a favorite hobby, rest, or relaxation. Anything will do as long as it is consciously absorbing. The purpose of all this is to allow the subconscious or preconscious to go to work on the impasse, unhampered by conscious control. It may be—as happened to May—that a critical resolution or clue or important missing variable will strike in the middle of a tennis game or while taking a nap. If such an insight does come in this way it is crucial for it to be recorded on paper—otherwise what drifted in from out of the blue may just drift out the same way. But whether or not a revelatory clue happens, we all can depend on the fact that the preconscious is working. Once we return again to conscious deliberation on the sermon-to-be, perhaps this time doing further exegetical work on the passage, the mind is somehow in a different place. The point here is that none of us can demand creativity, but the alternation of work and rest will maximize its possibility.

Sometimes it is helpful for creativity's sake to talk to someone not directly invested in the struggle. I recall vividly how on one occasion I was conducting a preaching workshop in which the first session was devoted to my homiletical theory or model. Then, boldly, I announced to the group of pastors that we would utilize the lectionary passages for the Sunday following our next session together, actually to generate a sermon. Together we looked up the lections for the Sunday and agreed to do our homework before the next session.

I don't know how much they worked on the passages, but I went home to the biblical struggle of my life. I read and reread the lections knowing full well that the final result would be the bottom-line payoff as to whether my homiletical method really works—or at least those pastors would think so! But it was clear—oh, so terribly clear—there was not the faintest hint of a sermon in any of those passages of Scripture, or all of them put together! The fact that my homiletical method was "on trial," so to speak, intensified the frustration of my mind's battle. I utilized the method I learned from Rollo May, but to no avail. The insight that should have come in out of the blue, stayed out! I was desperate, and I told my wife about my desperation as we traveled in the car out of town during a day in between the two workshop sessions. I told her my troubles, my panic, and just precisely how it was that we had happened on the most unpromising set of passages to be found in the three-year lectionary (and there are many unpromising sets to be found!).

It was as I began telling her what was *not there* that what *was there* began talking to me. Within a thirty-mile stretch of road I had more than enough ideas with which to work when the pastors met again!

All of which is to identify two more important factors relative to maximizing our creativity in sermon preparation time. One is the importance of talking to someone about the gestating sermon idea or text—long before a sermon begins to take shape. When we speak to a colleague or friend *too late* in the preparation process, their remarks will become either pale affirmation or irritating impediment. By that time it is too late to talk; it is better to just get up to the pulpit and preach. But early in the preparation process it is exceedingly helpful— even if you seem not to have any good ideas. The presence of a listener—even if the listener says little—is important precisely because we will tell another differently than we tell ourselves. As we couch our remarks to meet their particular personalities, our thoughts shift gears, become transformed, and energized. It is the dialogue of our telling and their listening that allows our preconscious the freedom it needs. Besides that, the listener may talk back—further enriching the possibilities of our creativity. Surely this must in part account for Browne Barr's preference in holding sermon preparation sessions with a group from the congregation *prior* to the preaching of the sermon, rather than a talk-back session after the sermon has been preached.

Even without someone to talk to regarding the sermon-to-be, one should talk the sermon ideas out loud—in the study, in the car on the way to a hospital visit, or wherever. Quite clearly, oral speech is different from silent thought. It has a different connection to the preconscious and literally a different grammar. These differences lie behind Clyde Fant's reminder to prepare "in the medium which will eventually be used."[12] Moreover, the story is profound that tells of the person rebuked by another to be silent until "you know what you want to say," and who responded: "How can I know what I want to say until I hear myself say it?" We all know the experience of sharing our views on an issue only to reject them once they are uttered—that experience Henri Bergson calls the "power of negation," when an image "breathes into his ear the word—*impossible!*" It is the veto voice of the preconscious that cannot be elicited well when we think only silently. Hence, factor number three: Prepare sermons out loud. To do so is to unleash the preconscious in creative ways.

A similar factor lies halfway between the first two. It is not only important to prepare out loud, and to talk with someone, it is also helpful to role-play pre-sermon thoughts. If there is a character in the biblical passage, have a chat with him or her. Or talk through an idea with a hypothetical parishioner while you sit alone in the study. Explain to this non-present parishioner what your sermonic goal is—what you hope to accomplish, or how difficult this particular passage is. Argue awhile with Jesus about that impossible admonition, take the side of the sermonic villain (such as the elder son in the prodigal son story) and defend *out loud* what up till now seemed an untenable position or piece of behavior. Remember how the villagers grumbled when Jesus announced to Zacchaeus in the tree and to them all that he was going to Zacchaeus' house for lunch? Well, what did they say? Say it out loud as you imagine it; it is just the opportunity your preconscious has been waiting for—to get a word in edgewise. Greater homiletical creativity likely will be the result.

Craddock warns us about our having been trained to think deductively when preaching—a most unnatural way. To role-play *any* conversation is to turn ideas around to inductive form. How often in a seminary preaching lab it occurs: The student preacher pronounces the gospel to us or makes an important point, which by placement in the sermonic process or even tone of voice is implied to be important but is utterly unclear to us, the listeners. In the evaluation session that follows someone will ask: "What did you mean when you said . . . ?" And the point is then made to us—clearly, even powerfully. To ask: "Why didn't you say that in the sermon?" is a cruel question, for it is now too late! Had the preacher utilized role-play "with us" prior to the actual preaching event, the preacher likely could have avoided the problem, and chances are that the sermon would have been far more creative.

Beyond Craddock's important advice regarding induction, which can be aided by role-play, is something else—just one step removed. It is free association. I believe that a form of free association (or something rather close to it) is as potentially important to sermon preparation as sometimes considered in psychiatric therapy. The principle at work when therapy is the context is to utilize an intentional method that can set the preconscious loose in the unintentional flow of free association. I recommend something quite similar for sermon preparation. When one is stymied in preparing a sermon and cannot seem to make heads or tails of an issue or a text, I suggest laying the pen aside, rising from the desk, and to commence talking. Say anything, let speech flow with its immediate nonsense. Soon it may turn to uncommon sense as the creative forces flow. If Polanyi is correct that "we know more than we can tell," it is quite possible that free association can be an important key toward finding out what is that "more."

Perhaps the most important factor maximizing creativity during sermon preparation time—at least the most heretical—is to begin writing a sermon before you are ready (or before you think you are ready). Over and over again(and as we have already noted) creative narrative artists speak of allowing the story to lead them, the characters, to determine the plot. This idea runs counter to how most of us were taught to prepare sermons. "Get your random ideas organized by means of an outline," I was told. "Get the framework, and fill in the blanks"—all of which means the end product is to be known *before* one begins. I was told even to summarize the gist of the sermon in one sentence, which was to be written on the top of the page of notes—so that it could reign majestically over the work. The result often is a painting-by-numbers!

The homiletical equivalent to "staying in the presence of the characters" or "listening to the story" is *not to know* the end product before one actually begins writing, but rather to go with the flow, become subservient to the energy of the "generative idea" as H. Grady Davis would call it,[18] and allow the energy of the idea to control the process. Such a process method maximizes preconscious activity and hence creativity.

The result may be startling—as I have in fact experienced in the writing of this very volume. The chapters here about which I thought I knew the most are the most pedantic in result, and conversely, those sections that have worried me most, the content of which I seemed to know least and felt least capable of writing have turned out to be the most creative. The process is clear to me as I reflect upon it: I would finally determine that I could not research the subject more and had just better begin somewhere—and one thing would lead to another, until finally I would read what I had written with utter surprise.

To a lesser degree this has been true in this very section. I had notes identifying the various factors I wanted to identify, but I purposely did not outline them in some rational order. I simply began with what I thought ought to be the beginning. In every case but one, I found myself entering the next section before completing the last and before examining my notes to see what "ought" to come next. The result is the following order of suggestions aimed at maximizing creativity in sermon preparation:

1. To alternate intensive work periods with other kinds of activity.
2. To talk with someone early in the preparation process.
3. To talk out loud to yourself.
4. To role-play the issue or scene.
5. To utilize free association at difficult points, and to
6. Commence writing before you are "ready."

Now, the above list is not ordered thematically, but rather it simply evolved—which compensates for lack of tight order by a better process flow. In addition, when I began, I had no intention to include such sources as Barr, Bergson, Craddock, Davis, or Polanyi. These sources came to mind while I was actually writing my suggestions.

Now perhaps the issue of creativity can be more formally ordered, namely that:

I. Creativity is not something a few people have, but rather a potential result we all possess to a considerable degree, and that

II. Although one cannot will directly to be creative, one can choose certain behaviors that will maximize creative powers waiting to be unleashed, and that

III. The key to creativity lies in releasing the creative preconscious mind from the controls of routine consciousness.

I propose the following behaviors toward greater creativity in sermon preparation time:

I. Alternate work with other activity.

II. Talk out loud
—with another person
—to oneself
—in role-playing
—by means of free association.

III. Write before you are "ready."

A final suggestion toward maximizing creativity: work over your head, so that you can work under your head.

Two kinds of reflection on one's own sermon work and that of others reinforce the importance of this point. First, preachers often tell me that it was not the sermon that most easily came that turned out the "best"—but quite the reverse. Called upon to use an unlikely text or address a difficult theme, preachers will sweat out what they know will be an "impossible sermon" with the result of "one of my best." Other times, sermon preparation will be "a breeze" and the sermons die stillborn. I trust I am not just alleging something similar to the notion that medicine must taste awful to be effective. I believe these reports best can be accounted for by noting that the easy-to-come-by sermon may be so because its simplicity allows quick conscious effort and little demand for preconscious impact. Sermons that highlight exhortation and imperative claim while minimizing analysis and gospel indicative often come quickly and accomplish little. It is when the theme is complicated and the answers difficult to find that homiletical sweat is evoked and preconscious agenda is born.

A kind of parallel observation arises frequently in the context of seminary preaching labs. The post-sermon discussion often reveals that the preacher's theology is in fact quite a bit more sophisticated and reflective than the sermon suggested. For example, the sermon presumed a high capacity for willpower and the listeners admonished to conscious effort. Later in the discussion we would discover the preacher really did not think our will so free nor the effort called for so possible. So how do you account for this discrepancy between the theology of the sermon and the theology of the sermonizer?

I think simply that the preacher's theology had been constantly impacted by preconscious knowledge of the untidy nature of human life—drawing perhaps from counseling work, the preacher's own life history, etc. But sermon time demanded clarity and yet provided limited preparation time in which to produce the clarity. The conscious mind was happy to oblige, and the result was a tidy sermon that concentrated on that tidy conscious facility of willpower. Meanwhile the preconscious was thwarted in doing its proper and creative work.

All of which is to suggest that maximizing creativity requires that we get in over our own heads, where the complexity of life leaves us dizzy and the gospel none too neat and tidy. Then we will be thrown into that bind that requires conscious effort and necessary time for preconscious mulling and sorting. Then that quality called creativity has its chance to emerge.

As we conclude our excursion into creativity it is worth noting how large looms *time*—and even timing. Note particularly that the importance of getting away from conscious sermon work is not just *that* it happen, but *when* it happens, that the effectiveness of talking to another about one's sermon ideas prior to the sermon itself is dependent upon *when* one talks, that for a sermon to be creative and also to be true to what we really believe takes *time* for preconscious forces to work. And all of us know the importance of timing as it relates to preparation and delivery—how some sermons seem over-prepared and flat, while others seem under-prepared and premature.

We live in *time*. Space, as a friend of mine put it, will never get us, but time will. Preparation time can become the opportunity for creativity to result, not in the sense of the gift of the few but in the larger sense of the creative capacities of us all. To use our preparation time well and hence to allow our creativity to flow can result in our knowing with joy what really is meant by "doing TIME in the pulpit."

NOTES

1. Sermon Time as the Ordering of Experience

1. Ilion T. Jones, *Principles and Practice of Preaching* (Nashville: Abingdon Press, 1956), p. 36.
2. J. Randall Nichols, *Building the Word* (San Francisco: Harper & Row, 1981).
3. Jones, *Principles and Practice of Preaching*, p.93.
4. Fred B. Craddock, *As One Without Authority* (Enid, Oklahoma: Phillips University Press, 1974), p. 56.
5. Henry Grady Davis, *Design for Preaching* (Philadelphia: Fortress Press, 1958), p. 15.
6. James S. Stewart, *The Strong Name* (New York: Scribner's, 1941), pp. 46th ff.
7. Edmund A. Steimle, Morris J. Niedenthal, and Charles L. Rice, *Preaching the Story* (Philadelphia: Fortress Press, 1980) pp.121-25.
8. Giles Gunn, "*Literature and its Relation to Religion*," *Journal of Religion*, Vol. 50, No. 3, July 1970, p. 283.
9. Personal interview, May 1, 1981.
10. Andrew W. Blackwood, *The Fine Art of Preaching* (New York: Macmillan, 1937), p. 146.
11. R. E. C. Browne, *The Ministry of the Word* (Philadelphia: Fortress Press, 1976), p. 15
12. Dan Otto Via, Jr., *The Parables* (Philadelphia: Fortress Press, 1967), p. 66.
13. Robert Roth, *Story and Reality* (Grand Rapids: Eerdmans, 1973), p. 96.

14. J. H. Jowett, *The Preacher: His Life and Work* (New York: Harper, 1912), p. 133.
15. Browne, *The Ministry of the Word*, p. 28.
16. Edwin Muir, *The Structure of the Novel* (London: 1928), p. 16.
17. Elizabeth Dipple, *Plot* (London: Methuen, 1970), p. 3.
18. Wesley A. Kort, *Narrative Elements and Religious Meaning* (Philadelphia: Fortress Press, 1975), p. 5, 12.
19. Steimle, Niedenthal, and Rice, *Preaching the Story*.
20. Frederick Buechner, *Telling the Truth* (New York: Harper, 1977), p. 4.

2. The Times of Our Life

1. Fredrick Jameson, *Satre: The Origins of Style*, in Margaret Church, *Time and Reality: Studies in Contemporary Fiction.* (Chapel Hill: The University of North Carolina Press, 1949), p. 260.
2. Thomas Mann, "The Magic Mountain," in Wyndham Lewis, *Time and Western Man* (Boston: Beacon Press, 1957), p. 131.
3. Hans Meyerhoff, *Time in Literature* (Berkeley: University of California Press, 1955), p. 1.
4. David G. Buttrick, reprinted by permission from *Interpretation.* Originally published in Volume XXXV, No. 1 (January 1981), p. 48.
5. Ibid., p. 49.
6. Robert Scholes and Robert Kellogg, *The Nature of Narrative* (London: Oxford University Press, 1966), p. 221.
7. Erich Frank, *Philosophical Understanding and Religious Truth* (London: Oxford University Press, 1945), p. 68.
8. Patricia Drechsel Tobin, *Time and the Novel* (Princeton: Princeton University Press, 1978), p. 12.
9. Norman Perrin, *The Kingdom of God in the Teaching of Jesus* (Philadelphia: Westminster Press, 1963), pp. 160-61.

10. John Dominic Crossan, *In Parables* (New York: Harper, 1973), p. 31.
11. Ibid., p. 23.
12. Steimle, Niedenthal, and Rice, *Preaching the Story*, p. 14.
13. Ibid., p. 13.
14. Edward T. Hall, *The Dance of Life* (Garden City, N.Y.: Anchor Press/Doubleday, 1983).

3. The Story's Time

1. Brian Wicker, *The Story-Shaped World* (London: The Athlone Press, 1975), p. 47.
2. In Kort, *Narrative Elements and Religious Meaning*, p. 84.
3. In L'Engle, *Walking on Water*, p. 84.
4. Lonnie D. Kliever, *The Shattered Spectrum* (Atlanta: John Knox Press, 1981), p. 156.
5. Amos Wilder, *The Language of the Gospel* (N. Y.: Harper and Row, 1964) p. 65.
6. Stephen D. Crites, "The Narrative Quality of Experience," *Journal of the American Academy of Religion*, (September 1971), p. 295.
7. Henry H. Mitchell, *The Recovery of Preaching* (San Francisco: Harper, 1977), p. 29.
8. Roth, *Story and Reality*, p. 152, 164, 165.
9. Kort, p. 43.
10. Craddock, *Overhearing the Gospel*, pp. 82-100.
11. Kort, *Narrative Elements and Religious Meaning*, p. 21.
12. Buechner, *Telling the Truth*, p. 58.
13. *The Poetry of Robert Frost*, edited by Edward Connery Lathem (New York: Holt, Rinehart and Winston, 1969), pp. 224-25.
14. Jones, *Principles and Practice of Preaching*, pp. 99, 105.
15. James L. Adams, *Conceptual Blockbusting*. (San Francisco: W. H. Freeman 1974), p. 15.
16. Kort, *Narrative Elements and Religious Meaning*, p. 40.

17. Browne, *The Ministry of the Word*, p. 27.
18. Joseph Fletcher, *Situation Ethics* (Philadelphia: Westminster Press, 1966), p. 13.
19. Eliseo Vivas, *Creation and Discovery* (Chicago 1955), p. 134.
20. Crites, "The Narrative Quality of Experience," p. 306.
21. Personal interview, May 1, 1981.
22. Kliever, *The Sheltered Spectrum*, p. 155.
23. Personal interview, May 1, 1981.
24. Helmut Thielicke, *The Trouble with the Church* (New York: Harper, 1965), pp. 3-6.

4. Narrative Time

1. Norman Perrin, *Jesus and the Language of the Kingdom.* (Philadelphia: Fortress Press, 1976), p. 50.

5. The Bible and Time

1. H. Richard Niebuhr, *The Meaning of Revelation* (New York: Macmillan, 1941), pp. 32-66.
2. Amos Wilder, *Theopoetic* (Philadelphia: Fortress Press, 1976), p. 1.
3. Browne, *The Ministry of the Word* p. 15.
4. Via, *The Parables,* p. 66.
5. In Browne, *The Ministry of the Word,* p. 86.
6. Amos Wilder, *Grace Confounding: Poems* (Philadelphia: Fortress Press, 1972), p. ix.
7. John Ciardi and Miller Williams, *How Does a Poem Mean?* (Boston: Houghton Mifflin, 1975), p. 10.
8. Buechner, *Telling the Truth,* p. 40.
9. Vivas, *Creation and Discovery,* pp. 116, 209.
10. Jerome S. Bruner, *On Knowing: Essays for the Left Hand* (Cambridge, Mass. Belknap Press, 1963).
11. Susanne Langer, *Philosophy in a New Key* (New York: New American Library Press, 1951), p. 89.
12. Kenneth E. Boulding, *The Image* (Ann Arbor, Michigan: The University of Michigan Press, 1961).

13. Gordon W. Allport, *Becoming* (New Haven: Yale University Press, 1955), p. 87.
14. Buechner, *Telling the Truth*, pp. 21, 22.
15. Sallie McFague TeSelle, *Speaking in Parables* (Philadelphia: Fortress Press, 1975), p. 5.
16. Charles E. Reagan and David Stewart, *The Philosophy of Paul Ricoeur* (Boston: Beacon Press, 1978), p. 233.
17. Perrin, *Jesus and the Language of the Kingdom*, p 73.
18. Wicker, *The Story-Shaped World*, p. 15.
19. Davis, *Design for Preaching*, p. 15.
20. Mitchell, *The Recovery of Preaching*, p. 32.
21. Personal interview May 1, 1981.

6. Preparation, Creativity, and Time

1. Personal interview May 1, 1981.
2. In L'Engle, *Walking on Water*, p. 72.
3. In Adams, *Conceptual Blockbusting*, p. 121.
4. George B. Leonard, *Education and Ecstasy* (New York: Dell Publishing Co. 1968), pp. 1, 120.
5. In Adams, *Conceptual Blockbusting*, p. 52.
6. Ibid., p. 121.
7. Ibid., p. 122.
8. Rollo May, *The Courage to Create* (Bantam Books, 1975), p. 137.
9. Adams, *Conceptual Blockbusting* p. 123.
10. May, *The Courage to Create*, p. 7, 66.
11. Ibid., p. 60.
12. Clyde E. Fant, *Preaching for Today* (New York: Harper, 1975), p. 120.
13. Davis, *Design for Preaching*, pp. 21 ff.